영어 원서로 읽는 셜록 1

A Study in Scarlet

영어 원서로 읽는 셜록 1 - A Study in Scarlet
Reading Sherlock without a Dictionary 1 - A Study in Scarlet (Korean Edition)
Sir Arthur Conan Doyle

펴낸곳: 북스트릿
주소: 서울시 은평구 연서로 17길 28-10 302호
원작: 아서 코난 도일 Arthur Conan Doyle
일러스트레이터: 리하르트 거트슈미트 Richard Gutschmidt
편집 및 주석: 신찬범
북커버 및 내지 디자인: 북스트릿
E-mail : invino70@gmail.com
Homepage: https://bookstreetpress.modoo.at
Blog : blog.naver.com/invino70
Youtube: https://bit.ly/2Lcav3m
Fax: 0504-405-6711
초판 1쇄 2019년 8월 20일

© 2019 북스트릿 BookStreet
북스트릿의 허락없는 이 책의 일부 또는 전부의 무단 복제, 전재, 발췌를 금합니다

ISBN: 979-11-965278-8-4   13740

영어 원서로 읽는 셜록 1
A Study in Scarlet

Sir Arthur Conan Doyle

북스트릿
BookStreet

머리말

    이 책은 영문 고전을 깊이 있게 이해하고 감상하기 위해 기획되었습니다.

    영어 원서를 읽는 데에 있어서 가장 큰 어려움 중 하나는 생소한 단어와 구 등을 매번 영어사전에서 찾아봐야 하는 번거로움입니다. 이러한 이유로 영어 원서의 독해가 쉽지 않은 것으로 인식되고 있으며, 특히 영어가 모국어가 아닌 분이나 영어를 공부하시는 분에게 어려움이 있습니다.

    본서는 이러한 어려움을 고려하여 영어 원서를 읽는 도중에 빈번하게 영어사전을 찾아봐야 하는 번거로움을 대폭 줄였으며, 영어사전을 될 수 있는 대로 적게 참조하면서 더 수월하게 영어 원서를 읽을 수 있게 했습니다.

    본서는 영문 고전의 원본 텍스트가 수록되어 있습니다. 문장 해석에 중요한 숙어, 구동사, 그 외 어려운 단어와 구 들을 선택하고 강조했습니다. 이들 단어와 구를 각 페이지 왼쪽에 단락별로 정의하고 설명했습니다 (대부분의 부사는 편의상 형용사 형태로 정의했습니다). 각 단어의 발음기호를 기재하여, 어휘력을 높이는 데 도움이 되게 했습니다. 스토리 흐름을 이해하기 위한 시놉시스를 책 말미에 추가했습니다. 또한 유튜브 https://bit.ly/2Lcav3m에서 오디오북을 들으실 수 있습니다.

    이 책이 독자분이 영문 고전을 읽는 데 의미 있는 도움이 되기를 바랍니다.

편집자

A Study in Scarlet

PART 1

1 Mr. Sherlock Holmes ··11

2 The Science of Deduction ······································28

3 The Lauriston Garden Mystery ······························50

4 What John Rance Had to Tell ································74

5 Our Advertisement Brings a Visitor ······················90

6 Tobias Gregson Shows What He Can Do ············105

7 Light in the Darkness ··126

PART 2

1 On the Great Alkali Plain ···149

2 The Flower of Utah ···171

3 John Ferrier Talks with the Prophet ································187

4 A Flight for Life···199

5 The Avenging Angels···220

6 A Continuation of the Reminiscences of John Watson, M.D.···240

7 The Conclusion ···265

주홍색 연구 시놉시스 ·· 278

PART I

Being a Reprint from the Reminiscences of John H. Watson, M.D., Late of the Army Medical Department

1 Mr. Sherlock Holmes

prescribe [priskráib] v.
규정하다
regiment [rédʒəmənt] n.
연대(聯隊)
pass [pæs, pɑːs] n.
협로, 산길, 고개, 통로

In the year 1878 I took my degree of Doctor of Medicine of the University of London, and proceeded to Netley to go through the course **prescribed** for surgeons in the army. Having completed my studies there, I was duly attached to the Fifth Northumberland Fusiliers as assistant surgeon. The **regiment** was stationed in India at the time, and before I could join it, the second Afghan war had broken out. On landing at Bombay, I learned that my corps had advanced through the **passes**, and was already deep in the enemy's country. I followed,

campaign [kæmpéin] n.
전투
brigade [brigéid] n.
여단 (旅團)
subclavian [sʌbkléiviən] adj. 쇄골 아래의
ghazi [gάːziː] n.
회교도 전사
Had it not been for ~:
If it had not been for ~
orderly [ɔ́ːrdərli] n.
장교에게 딸린 부하병사

rally [rǽli] v.
회복하다

however, with many other officers who were in the same situation as myself, and succeeded in reaching Candahar in safety, where I found my regiment, and at once entered upon my new duties.

The **campaign** brought honours and promotion to many, but for me it had nothing but misfortune and disaster. I was removed from my **brigade** and attached to the Berkshires, with whom I served at the fatal battle of Maiwand. There I was struck on the shoulder by a Jezail bullet, which shattered the bone and grazed the **subclavian** artery. I should have fallen into the hands of the murderous **Ghazis had it not been for** the devotion and courage shown by Murray, my **orderly**, who threw me across a pack-horse, and succeeded in bringing me safely to the British lines.

Worn with pain, and weak from the prolonged hardships which I had undergone, I was removed, with a great train of wounded sufferers, to the base hospital at Peshawar. Here I **rallied**, and had already improved so far as to be able to walk about the wards, and even

bask [bæsk] v.
일광욕하다, 볕을 쬐다
enteric fever [entérik fíːvər] n.
장티푸스
convalescent [kɑ̀nvəlésnt / kɔ̀n-] adj.
회복기의
emaciate [iméiʃièit] v.
야위다, 마르다

to **bask** a little upon the verandah, when I was struck down by **enteric fever**, that curse of our Indian possessions. For months my life was despaired of, and when at last I came to myself and became **convalescent**, I was so weak and **emaciated** that a medical board determined that not a day should be lost in sending me back to England. I was dispatched, accordingly, in the troopship *Orontes*, and

There I was struck on the shoulder by a Jezail bullet, ... I should have fallen into the hands of the murderous Ghazis had it not been for the devotion and courage shown by Murray...

jetty [dʒéti] n.
부두, 방파제
irretrievable [ìritríːvəbəl] adj. 돌이킬 수 없는, 회복할 수 없는
paternal government: 권위주의 정부
kith and kin [kiθ -] n. 일가친척
gravitate [ɡrǽvətèit] v. 이끌리다, 하강하다
rusticate [rʌ́stəkèit] v. 시골로 가다
quarters [kwɔ́ːrtər] n. 숙소
pretentious [priténʃəs] adj. 과시적인, 과장된, 허세의

landed a month later on Portsmouth **jetty**, with my health **irretrievably** ruined, but with permission from **a paternal government** to spend the next nine months in attempting to improve it.

I had **neither kith nor kin** in England, and was therefore as free as air—or as free as an income of eleven shillings and sixpence a day will permit a man to be. Under such circumstances, I naturally **gravitated** to London, that great cesspool into which all the loungers and idlers of the Empire are irresistibly drained. There I stayed for some time at a private hotel in the Strand, leading a comfortless, meaningless existence, and spending such money as I had, considerably more freely than I ought. So alarming did the state of my finances become, that I soon realized that I must either leave the metropolis and **rusticate** somewhere in the country, or that I must make a complete alteration in my style of living. Choosing the latter alternative, I began by making up my mind to leave the hotel, and to take up my **quarters** in some less **pretentious** and less expensive domicile.

dresser [drésər] n.
외과수술 조수
wilderness [wíldə:rnis] n.
황무지
crony [króuni] n.
친구
hansom [hǽnsəm] n.
2륜마차

rattle [rǽtl] v.
덜걱거리다
lath [læθ, lɑ:θ] n.
외, 욋가지(지붕이나 벽에 흙을 바르기 위해 엮어 넣는 가느다란 나뭇가지)

On the very day that I had come to this conclusion, I was standing at the Criterion Bar, when someone tapped me on the shoulder, and turning round I recognized young Stamford, who had been a **dresser** under me at Barts. The sight of a friendly face in the great **wilderness** of London is a pleasant thing indeed to a lonely man. In old days Stamford had never been a particular **crony** of mine, but now I hailed him with enthusiasm, and he, in his turn, appeared to be delighted to see me. In the exuberance of my joy, I asked him to lunch with me at the Holborn, and we started off together in a **hansom**.

"Whatever have you been doing with yourself, Watson?" he asked in undisguised wonder, as we **rattled** through the crowded London streets. "You are as thin as a **lath** and as brown as a nut."

I gave him a short sketch of my adventures, and had hardly concluded it by the time that we reached our destination.

"Poor devil!" he said, commiseratingly, after he had listened to my misfortunes. "What are you up to now?"

as to ~: ~에 관하여

bemoan [bimóun] v.
슬퍼하다, 한탄하다

By Jove:
놀람, 강조 등을 나타내
는 감탄사, Jove는 로마신
Jupiter의 다른 이름임

"Looking for lodgings." I answered. "Trying to solve the problem **as to** whether it is possible to get comfortable rooms at a reasonable price."

"That's a strange thing," remarked my companion; "you are the second man today that has used that expression to me."

"And who was the first?" I asked.

"A fellow who is working at the chemical laboratory up at the hospital. He was **bemoaning** himself this morning because he could not get someone to go halves with him in some nice rooms which he had found, and which were too much for his purse."

"**By Jove!**" I cried, "if he really wants someone to share the rooms and the expense, I am the very man for him. I should prefer having a partner to being alone."

Young Stamford looked rather strangely at me over his wineglass. "You don't know Sherlock Holmes yet," he said; "perhaps you would not care for him as a constant companion."

"Why, what is there against him?"

queer [kwiər] adj.
괴상한, 이상야릇한
decent [díːsənt] adj.
고상한, 기품있는

go in for something:
do something regularly, or
enjoy something
anatomy [ənǽtəmi] n.
해부학
desultory [désəltɔ̀ːri] adj.
엉뚱한, 종잡을 수 없는
amass [əmǽs] v.
모으다, 축적하다

"You don't know Sherlock Holmes yet," he said; "perhaps you would not care for him as a constant companion."

studious [stjúːdiəs] adj.
학구적인, 열심히 하는

"Oh, I didn't say there was anything against him. He is a little **queer** in his ideas—an enthusiast in some branches of science. As far as I know he is a **decent** fellow enough."

"A medical student, I suppose?" said I.

"No—I have no idea what he intends to **go in for**. I believe he is well up in **anatomy**, and he is a first-class chemist; but, as far as I know, he has never taken out any systematic medical classes. His studies are very **desultory** and eccentric, but he has **amassed** a lot of out-of-the-way knowledge which would astonish his professors."

"Did you never ask him what he was going in for?" I asked.

"No; he is not a man that it is easy to draw out, though he can be communicative enough when the fancy seizes him."

"I should like to meet him," I said. "If I am to lodge with anyone, I should prefer a man of **studious** and quiet habits. I am not strong enough yet to stand much noise or excitement. I had enough of both in Afghanistan to last me for the remainder of my natural existence. How could I meet this friend of yours?"

"He is sure to be at the laboratory," returned my companion. "He either avoids the place for weeks, or else he works there from morning till night. If you like, we will drive round together after luncheon."

"Certainly," I answered, and the conversation drifted away into other channels.

As we made our way to the hospital after leaving the Holborn, Stamford gave me a few more particulars about the gentleman whom I proposed to take as a fellow-lodger.

"You mustn't blame me if you don't **get on with** him," he said; "I know nothing more of him than I have learned from meeting him occasionally in the laboratory. You proposed this arrangement, so you must not hold me responsible."

"If we don't get on it will be easy to part company," I answered. "It seems to me, Stamford," I added, looking hard at my companion, "that you have some reason for washing your hands of the matter. Is this fellow's **temper** so **formidable**, or what is it? Don't be **mealymouthed** about it."

---

get on with someone:
잘 지내다. 친하게 지내다

temper [témpə:r] n.
기질, 성미
formidable [fɔ́:rmidəb-əl] adj. 험난한, 무서운
mealymouthed [míːli-máuðd] adj.
말뿐인, 에둘러 말하는

inexpressible [ìniksprésəbəl] adj. 표현할 수 없는, 형언할 수 없는
malevolence [məlévələns] n. 악의, 증오
do justice to : 정당하게 다루다, 제대로 대하다

bizarre [bizά:r] adj. 기괴한, 별난

"It is not easy to express the **inexpressible**," he answered with a laugh. "Holmes is a little too scientific for my tastes—it approaches to cold-bloodedness. I could imagine his giving a friend a little pinch of the latest vegetable alkaloid, not out of **malevolence**, you understand, but simply out of a spirit of inquiry in order to have an accurate idea of the effects. To **do him justice**, I think that he would take it himself with the same readiness. He appears to have a passion for definite and exact knowledge."

"Very right too."

"Yes, but it may be pushed to excess. When it comes to beating the subjects in the dissecting-rooms with a stick, it is certainly taking rather a **bizarre** shape."

"Beating the subjects!"

"Yes, to verify how far bruises may be produced after death. I saw him at it with my own eyes."

"And yet you say he is not a medical student?"

"No. Heaven knows what the objects of his studies are. But here we are, and you must form your own impressions about

vista [vístə] n.
전망, 조망

bristle [brís-əl] v.
가득차다
retort [ritɔ́:rt] n.
증류기
reagent [ri:éidʒ-ənt] n.
시약(試藥)
Had he discovered ~:
If he had discovered ~

him." As he spoke, we turned down a narrow lane and passed through a small side-door, which opened into a wing of the great hospital. It was familiar ground to me, and I needed no guiding as we ascended the bleak stone staircase and made our way down the long corridor with its **vista** of whitewashed wall and dun-coloured doors. Near the farther end a low arched passage branched away from it and led to the chemical laboratory.

This was a lofty chamber, lined and littered with countless bottles. Broad, low tables were scattered about, which **bristled** with **retorts**, test-tubes, and little Bunsen lamps, with their blue flickering flames. There was only one student in the room, who was bending over a distant table absorbed in his work. At the sound of our steps he glanced round and sprang to his feet with a cry of pleasure. "I've found it! I've found it," he shouted to my companion, running towards us with a test-tube in his hand. "I have found a **re-agent** which is precipitated by haemoglobin, and by nothing else." **Had he**

1 Mr. Sherlock Holmes

discovered a gold mine, greater delight could not have shone upon his features.

"Dr. Watson, Mr. Sherlock Holmes," said Stamford, introducing us.

"How are you?" he said **cordially**, gripping my hand with a strength for which I should hardly have given him credit. "You have been in Afghanistan, I **perceive**."

"How on earth did you know that?" I asked in astonishment.

"Never mind," said he, **chuckling** to himself. "The question now is about haemoglobin. No doubt you see the significance of this discovery of mine?"

"It is interesting, chemically, no doubt," I answered, "but practically——"

"Why, man, it is the most practical medico-legal discovery for years. Don't you see that it gives us an **infallible** test for blood stains. Come over here now!" He seized me by the coat-sleeve in his eagerness, and drew me over to the table at which he had been working. "Let us have some fresh blood," he said, digging a long **bodkin** into his finger, and drawing off the resulting drop of blood in a chemical pipette. "Now, I add this small

---

cordially [kɔ́:rdʒəli] adv.
진심으로, 성심껏
perceive [pərsí:v] v.
알아차리다, 이해하다

chuckle [tʃʌ́kl] v.
소리없이 웃다

infallible [infǽləbəl] adj.
확실한, 절대 옳은
bodkin [bɑ́dkin] n.
송곳, 바늘

quantity of blood to a litre of water. You perceive that the resulting mixture has the appearance of pure water. The proportion of blood cannot be more than one in a million. I have no doubt, however, that we shall be able to obtain the characteristic reaction." As he spoke, he threw into the vessel a few white crystals, and then added some drops of a transparent fluid. In an instant the contents

"You have been in Afghanistan, I perceive."

precipitate [prisípətèit] v. 침전시키다, 떨어뜨리다	assumed a dull mahogany colour, and a brownish dust was **precipitated** to the bottom of the glass jar.

"Ha! ha!" he cried, clapping his hands, and looking as delighted as a child with a new toy. "What do you think of that?"

"It seems to be a very **delicate** test," I remarked.

"Beautiful! beautiful! The old Guaiacum test was very **clumsy** and uncertain. So is the microscopic examination for blood corpuscles. The latter is valueless if the stains are a few hours old. Now, this appears to act as well whether the blood is old or new. **Had this test been invented**, there are hundreds of men now walking the earth who would long ago have paid the penalty of their crimes."

"Indeed!" I **murmured**.

"Criminal cases are continually **hinging upon** that one point. A man is suspected of a crime months perhaps after it has been committed. His linen or clothes are examined, and brownish stains discovered upon them. Are they blood stains, or mud stains, or rust stains, or fruit stains, or what are they? That is a question which

---

delicate [délikət, -kit] adj. 세련된, 고상한, 섬세한

clumsy [klʌ́mzi] adj. 서투른, 어색한, 투박한

Had this test been invented: If this test had been invented

murmur [mə́:rmə:r] v. 낮게 속삭이다, 중얼거리다

hinge on/upon something: depend on something, or need something in order to be successful
~이 중요하다

has puzzled many an expert, and why? Because there was no reliable test. Now we have the Sherlock Holmes' test, and there will no longer be any difficulty."

His eyes fairly **glittered** as he spoke, and he put his hand over his heart and bowed as if to some applauding crowd **conjured up** by his imagination.

"You are to be congratulated," I remarked, considerably surprised at his enthusiasm.

"There was the case of Von Bischoff at Frankfort last year. He would certainly have been hung **had this test been in existence**. Then there was Mason of Bradford, and the notorious Muller, and Lefevre of Montpellier, and Samson of New Orleans. I could name a score of cases in which it would have been decisive."

"You seem to be a walking calendar of crime," said Stamford with a laugh. "You might start a paper on those lines. Call it the 'Police News of the Past.'"

"Very interesting reading it might be made, too," remarked Sherlock Holmes, sticking a small piece of **plaster** over the prick on his finger. "I have to be

dabble [dǽbəl] v.
(물 등을) 튀기다
mottle [mátl / mɔ́tl] v.
얼룩덜룩하게 하다

diggings/digs [dígiŋ] n.
주거, 숙소

by no means:
절대 아닌
in the dumps:
의기소침하여, 울적하여

careful," he continued, turning to me with a smile, "for I **dabble** with poisons a good deal." He held out his hand as he spoke, and I noticed that it was all **mottled** over with similar pieces of plaster, and discoloured with strong acids.

"We came here on business," said Stamford, sitting down on a high three-legged stool, and pushing another one in my direction with his foot. "My friend here wants to take **diggings**, and as you were complaining that you could get no one to go halves with you, I thought that I had better bring you together."

Sherlock Holmes seemed delighted at the idea of sharing his rooms with me. "I have my eye on a suite in Baker Street," he said, "which would suit us down to the ground. You don't mind the smell of strong tobacco, I hope?"

"I always smoke 'ship's' myself," I answered.

"That's good enough. I generally have chemicals about, and occasionally do experiments. Would that annoy you?"

"**By no means.**"

"Let me see—what are my other shortcomings. I get **in the dumps** at times, and

on end: 계속해서, 끊임없이 sulky [sʌ́lki]: adj. 뚱한, 부루퉁한	don't open my mouth for days **on end**. You must not think I am **sulky** when I do that. Just let me alone, and I'll soon be right. What have you to confess now? It's just as well for two fellows to know the worst of one another before they begin to live together."

I laughed at this **cross-examination**. "I keep a bull pup," I said, "and I object to **rows** because my nerves are shaken, and I get up at all sorts of **ungodly** hours, and I am extremely lazy. I have another set of vices when I'm well, but those are the principal ones at present."

cross-examination [krɔːsˈigzæmənéiʃən] n.
반대심문
row [rau] n.
소음, 아우성
ungodly [ʌngʌ́dli / -gɔ́d-] adj. 지독한, 터무니없는

"Do you include violin playing in your **category** of rows?" he asked, anxiously.

"It depends on the player," I answered. "A well-played violin is a **treat** for the gods—a badly played one——"

category [kǽtəgɔ̀ːri / -gəri] n.
종류, 범주
treat [triːt] n.
기쁨, 대접

"Oh, that's all right," he cried, with a merry laugh. "I think we may consider the thing as settled—that is, if the rooms are agreeable to you."

"When shall we see them?"

"I have my eye on a suite in Baker Street," he said, "which would suit us down to the ground…"

"Call for me here at noon to-morrow, and we'll go together and settle everything," he answered.

"All right—noon exactly," said I, shaking his hand.

We left him working among his chemicals, and we walked together towards my hotel.

"By the way," I asked suddenly, stopping and turning upon Stamford, "how **the deuce** did he know that I had come from Afghanistan?"

My companion smiled an **enigmatical** smile. "That's just his little peculiarity," he said. "A good many people have wanted to know how he finds things out."

"Oh! a mystery is it?" I cried, rubbing my hands. "This is very **piquant**. I am much **obliged** to you for bringing us together. 'The proper study of mankind is man,' you know."

"You must study him, then," Stamford said, as he bade me good-bye. "You'll find him a **knotty** problem, though. I'll **wager** he learns more about you than you about him. Good-bye."

"Good-bye," I answered, and strolled on to my hotel, considerably interested in my new **acquaintance**.

2 The Science of Deduction

on/upon the spot:
그 자리에서, 즉석에서

We met next day as he had arranged, and inspected the rooms at No. 221B, Baker Street, of which he had spoken at our meeting. They consisted of a couple of comfortable bed-rooms and a single large airy sitting-room, cheerfully furnished, and illuminated by two broad windows. So desirable in every way were the apartments, and so moderate did the terms seem when divided between us, that the bargain was concluded **upon the spot**, and we at once entered into possession. That very evening

portmanteau [pɔːrtmǽn-tou] n.
가죽 트렁크

invariable [invέəriəbəl] adj. 변화없는, 불변의
now and again: 때때로, 가끔, 이따금
utter [ʌ́tər] v. 말하다, 이야기하다

I moved my things round from the hotel, and on the following morning Sherlock Holmes followed me with several boxes and **portmanteaus**. For a day or two we were busily employed in unpacking and laying out our property to the best advantage. That done, we gradually began to settle down and to accommodate ourselves to our new surroundings.

Holmes was certainly not a difficult man to live with. He was quiet in his ways, and his habits were regular. It was rare for him to be up after ten at night, and he had **invariably** breakfasted and gone out before I rose in the morning. Sometimes he spent his day at the chemical laboratory, sometimes in the dissecting-rooms, and occasionally in long walks, which appeared to take him into the lowest portions of the City. Nothing could exceed his energy when the working fit was upon him; but **now and again** a reaction would seize him, and for days on end he would lie upon the sofa in the sitting-room, hardly **uttering** a word or moving a muscle from morning to night. On these occasions I have

narcotic [nɑːrkátik] n.
마약
temperance [témp-ərəns]
n. 중용, 절도

save [seiv] prep.
~을 제외하고
torpor [tɔ́ːrpər] n.
무기력, 무감각
fragile [frǽdʒəl / -dʒail]
adj. 허약한, 깨지기 쉬운, 섬세한

noticed such a dreamy, vacant expression in his eyes, that I might have suspected him of being addicted to the use of some **narcotic**, had not the **temperance** and cleanliness of his whole life forbidden such a notion.

As the weeks went by, my interest in him and my curiosity as to his aims in life gradually deepened and increased. His very person and appearance were such as to strike the attention of the most casual observer. In height he was rather over six feet, and so excessively lean that he seemed to be considerably taller. His eyes were sharp and piercing, **save** during those intervals of **torpor** to which I have alluded; and his thin, hawk-like nose gave his whole expression an air of alertness and decision. His chin, too, had the prominence and squareness which mark the man of determination. His hands were invariably blotted with ink and stained with chemicals, yet he was possessed of extraordinary delicacy of touch, as I frequently had occasion to observe when I watched him manipulating his **fragile** philosophical instruments.

set down:
생각하다, 간주하다
busybody [bízibàdi / -bɔ̀di]
n. 참견쟁이
reticence [rétəs-əns] n.
과묵함, 입이 무거움
genial [dʒíːnjəl] adj.
온화한, 다정한
monotony [mənátəni / -nɔ́t-] n.
지루함, 단조로움
hail [heil] v.
환영하다, 갈채하다
unravel [ʌnrǽvəl] v.
풀다, 해결하다

portal [pɔ́ːrtl] n.
대문, 입구
zeal [ziːl] n.
열심, 열의

2 The Science of Deduction   31

The reader may **set** me **down** as a hopeless **busybody**, when I confess how much this man stimulated my curiosity, and how often I endeavoured to break through the **reticence** which he showed on all that concerned himself. Before pronouncing judgment, however, be it remembered, how objectless was my life, and how little there was to engage my attention. My health forbade me from venturing out unless the weather was exceptionally **genial**, and I had no friends who would call upon me and break the **monotony** of my daily existence. Under these circumstances, I eagerly **hailed** the little mystery which hung around my companion, and spent much of my time in endeavouring to **unravel** it.

He was not studying medicine. He had himself, in reply to a question, confirmed Stamford's opinion upon that point. Neither did he appear to have pursued any course of reading which might fit him for a degree in science or any other recognized **portal** which would give him an entrance into the learned world. Yet his **zeal** for certain studies was remarkable, and within eccentric

ample [ǽmpl] adj.
풍부한, 충분한
astound [əstáund] v.
놀래키다
desultory [désəltɔ̀:ri] adj.
막연한, 종잡을 수 없는, 엉뚱한

limits his knowledge was so extraordinarily **ample** and minute that his observations have fairly **astounded** me. Surely no man would work so hard or attain such precise information unless he had some definite end in view. **Desultory** readers are seldom remarkable for the exactness of their learning. No man burdens his mind with small matters unless he has some very good reason for doing so.

His ignorance was as remarkable as his knowledge. Of contemporary literature, philosophy and politics he appeared to know next to nothing. Upon my quoting Thomas Carlyle, he inquired in the naivest way who he might be and what he had done. My surprise reached a climax, however, when I found incidentally that he was ignorant of the Copernican Theory and of the composition of the Solar System. That any civilized human being in this nineteenth century should not be aware that the earth travelled round the sun appeared to me to be such an extraordinary fact that I could hardly realize it.

"You appear to be astonished," he said, smiling at my expression of surprise.

get crowded out:
밀려나다
jumble [dʒʌ́mbəl] v.
뒤범벅이 되다
distend [disténd] v.
늘어나다
depend on (upon) it:
확실히, 틀림없이, 반드시
elbow out:
밀어내다

"Now that I do know it I shall do my best to forget it."

"To forget it!"

"You see," he explained, "I consider that a man's brain originally is like a little empty attic, and you have to stock it with such furniture as you choose. A fool takes in all the lumber of every sort that he comes across, so that the knowledge which might be useful to him **gets crowded out**, or at best is **jumbled** up with a lot of other things, so that he has a difficulty in laying his hands upon it. Now the skilful workman is very careful indeed as to what he takes into his brain-attic. He will have nothing but the tools which may help him in doing his work, but of these he has a large assortment, and all in the most perfect order. It is a mistake to think that that little room has elastic walls and can **distend** to any extent. **Depend upon it** there comes a time when for every addition of knowledge you forget something that you knew before. It is of the highest importance, therefore, not to have useless facts **elbowing out** the useful ones."

"But the Solar System!" I protested.

"What the deuce is it to me?" he interrupted impatiently: "you say that we go round the sun. If we went round the moon it would not make a pennyworth of difference to me or to my work."

I was on the point of asking him what that work might be, but something in his manner showed me that the question would be an unwelcome one. I **pondered** over our short conversation, however, and endeavoured to draw my **deductions** from it. He said that he would acquire no knowledge which did not **bear upon** his object. Therefore all the knowledge which he possessed was such as would be useful to him. I **enumerated** in my own mind all the various points upon which he had shown me that he was exceptionally well informed. I even took a pencil and **jotted** them down. I could not help smiling at the document when I had completed it. It ran in this way:

Sherlock Holmes—his limits

---

ponder [pándər / pɔ́n-] v.
숙고하다, 곰곰 생각하다
deduction [didʌ́kʃən] n.
추론, 추리, 연역
bear upon:
관계되다
enumerate [injúːmərèit] v.
열거하다, 나열하다
jot [dʒɑt / dʒɔt] v.
간결하게 적다, 간단히 메모하다

"Now the skilful workman is very careful indeed as to what he takes into his brain-attic..."

nil [nil] n.
없음, 제로
astronomy [əstránəmi /
-trɔ́n-] n.
천문학
botany [bátəni / bɔ́t-] n.
식물학
geology [ʤiːáləʤi / ʤiɔ́l-]
n. 지질학
anatomy [ənǽtəmi] n.
해부학
perpetrate [pə́ːrpətrèit] v.
범하다, 저지르다
singlestick [síŋgəlstìk] n.
목검술

1. Knowledge of Literature.—**Nil**.
2.   Philosophy.—Nil.
3.   **Astronomy**.—Nil.
4.   Politics.—Feeble.
5   **Botany**.—Variable.
Well up in belladonna, opium, and poisons generally. Knows nothing of practical gardening.
6. Knowledge of **Geology**.— Practical, but limited.
Tells at a glance different soils from each other. After walks has shown me splashes upon his trousers, and told me by their colour and consistence in what part of London he had received them.
7. Knowledge of Chemistry. —Profound.
8.   **Anatomy**.—Accurate, but unsystematic.
9.   Sensational Literature.—Immense.
He appears to know every detail of every horror **perpetrated** in the century.
10. Plays the violin well.
11. Is an expert **singlestick** player, boxer, and swordsman.
12. Has a good practical knowledge of British law.

reconcile [rékənsàil] v.
조화시키다
calling [kɔ́:liŋ] n.
직업
may/might as well:
~하는 게 좋겠다.

allude [əlú:d] v.
언급하다, 암시하다
piece [pi:s] n.
예술 작품
Lied [li:d] (pl. Lieder [líːdər]) n.
가곡
air [ɛər] n.
멜로디, 선율
scrape [skreip] v.
문지르다, 스치다
fiddle [fídl] n.
바이올린
sonorous [sənɔ́:rəs, sɑ́nə-] adj. 울려퍼지는
melancholy [mélənkɑ̀li / -kɔ̀li] adj.
구슬픈, 울적한

When I had got so far in my list I threw it into the fire in despair. "If I can only find what the fellow is driving at by **reconciling** all these accomplishments, and discovering a **calling** which needs them all," I said to myself, "I **may as well** give up the attempt at once."

I see that I have **alluded** above to his powers upon the violin. These were very remarkable, but as eccentric as all his other accomplishments. That he could play **pieces**, and difficult pieces, I knew well, because at my request he has played me some of Mendelssohn's **Lieder**, and other favourites. When left to himself, however, he would seldom produce any music or attempt any recognized **air**. Leaning back in his armchair of an evening, he would close his eyes and **scrape** carelessly at the **fiddle** which was thrown across his knee. Sometimes the chords were **sonorous** and **melancholy**. Occasionally they were fantastic and cheerful. Clearly they reflected the thoughts which possessed him, but whether the music aided those thoughts, or whether the playing was simply the

2 The Science of Deduction

whim [hwim] n.
변덕
exasperate [igzǽspərèit] v.
격노하다, 분개하다
had it not been that:
if it had not been that

result of a **whim** or fancy was more than I could determine. I might have rebelled against these **exasperating** solos **had it not been that** he usually terminated them by playing in quick succession a whole series of my favourite airs as a slight compensation for the trial upon my patience.

During the first week or so we had no callers, and I had begun to think that my companion was as friendless a man

Leaning back in his armchair of an evening, he would close his eyes and scrape carelessly at the fiddle which was thrown across his knee.

sallow [sǽlou] adj.
창백한
seedy [síːdi] adj.
허름한
slipshod [ˈʃɑd / ˈʃɔd] adj.
단정치 못한, 되는 대로의
nondescript [nàndiskrípt/ nɔ̀ndiskrípt] adj.
막연한, 알 수 없는

as I was myself. Presently, however, I found that he had many acquaintances, and those in the most different classes of society. There was one little **sallow** rat-faced, dark-eyed fellow who was introduced to me as Mr. Lestrade, and who came three or four times in a single week. One morning a young girl called, fashionably dressed, and stayed for half an hour or more. The same afternoon brought a grey-headed, **seedy** visitor, looking like a Jew peddler, who appeared to me to be much excited, and who was closely followed by a **slipshod** elderly woman. On another occasion an old white-haired gentleman had an interview with my companion; and on another a railway porter in his velveteen uniform. When any of these **nondescript** individuals put in an appearance, Sherlock Holmes used to beg for the use of the sitting-room, and I would retire to my bedroom. He always apologized to me for putting me to this inconvenience. "I have to use this room as a place of business," he said, "and these people are my clients." Again I had an opportunity of

2 The Science of Deduction

point-blank [pɔ́intblǽŋk] adj. 솔직한, 노골적인
delicacy [délikəsi] n. 섬세함, 배려
confide [kənfáid] v. 비밀을 털어놓다, 개인 일을 이야기하다
of one's own accord: 자발적으로, 스스로의 선택에 의해
petulance [pétʃələns] n. 언짢음
curt [kə:rt] adj. 무뚝뚝한, 퉁명한
intimation [ìntəméiʃən] n. 통보
while away: 시간 등을 보내다

asking him a **point-blank** question, and again my **delicacy** prevented me from forcing another man to **confide** in me. I imagined at the time that he had some strong reason for not alluding to it, but he soon dispelled the idea by coming round to the subject **of his own accord**.

It was upon the 4th of March, as I have good reason to remember, that I rose somewhat earlier than usual, and found that Sherlock Holmes had not yet finished his breakfast. The landlady had become so accustomed to my late habits that my place had not been laid nor my coffee prepared. With the unreasonable **petulance** of mankind I rang the bell and gave a **curt intimation** that I was ready. Then I picked up a magazine from the table and attempted to **while away** the time with it, while my companion munched silently at his toast. One of the articles had a pencil mark at the heading, and I naturally began to run my eye through it.

Its somewhat ambitious title was *The Book of Life*, and it attempted to show how much an observant man might learn by

farfetched [fɑːrfétʃt] adj.
무리한, 억지의
twitch [twitʃ] n.
경련
fathom [fǽðəm] v.
알아내다, 추측하다
infallible [infǽləbəl] adj.
확실한, 절대 옳은
uninitiated [ʌ̀niníʃièitid] n.
초심자(들), 초보자(들)
necromancer [nékrəmæ̀nsəːr] n.
마법사, 점쟁이

infer [infə́ːr] v.
추론하다, 추리하다

an accurate and systematic examination of all that came in his way. It struck me as being a remarkable mixture of shrewdness and of absurdity. The reasoning was close and intense, but the deductions appeared to me to be **farfetched** and exaggerated. The writer claimed by a momentary expression, a **twitch** of a muscle or a glance of an eye, to **fathom** a man's inmost thoughts. Deceit, according to him, was an impossibility in the case of one trained to observation and analysis. His conclusions were as **infallible** as so many propositions of Euclid. So startling would his results appear to the **uninitiated** that until they learned the processes by which he had arrived at them they might well consider him as a **necromancer**.

"From a drop of water," said the writer, "a logician could **infer** the possibility of an Atlantic or a Niagara without having seen or heard of one or the other. So all life is a great chain, the nature of which is known whenever we are shown a single link of it. Like all other arts, the Science of Deduction and Analysis is one which

attain [ətéin] v.
얻다, 달성하다
puerile [pjúːəril, -ràil] adj.
유치한, 미숙한
callosity [kəlásəti / -lɔ́s-] n.
피부의 못, 굳어진 피부
expression [ikspréʃən] n.
얼굴, 표정
inconceivable [ìnkən-síːvəbəl] adj.
상상도 할 수 없는, 믿을 수 없는

can only be acquired by long and patient study, nor is life long enough to allow any mortal to **attain** the highest possible perfection in it. Before turning to those moral and mental aspects of the matter which present the greatest difficulties, let the inquirer begin by mastering more elementary problems. Let him, on meeting a fellow-mortal, learn at a glance to distinguish the history of the man, and the trade or profession to which he belongs. **Puerile** as such an exercise may seem, it sharpens the faculties of observation, and teaches one where to look and what to look for. By a man's finger nails, by his coat-sleeve, by his boot, by his trouser knees, by the **callosities** of his forefinger and thumb, by his **expression**, by his shirt cuffs—by each of these things a man's calling is plainly revealed. That all united should fail to enlighten the competent inquirer in any case is almost **inconceivable**."

ineffable [inéfəbəl] adj.
형언할 수 없는, 말로 표현할 수 없는
twaddle [twɑ́d-əl / twɔ́d-əl]
n. 쓸데없는 소리, 잡담

"What **ineffable twaddle**!" I cried, slapping the magazine down on the table; "I never read such rubbish in my life."

"What is it?" asked Sherlock Holmes.

seclusion [siklú:ʒ-ən] n.
은둔, 격리
lay [lei] v.
내기하다, ~에 걸다

"Why, this article," I said, pointing at it with my eggspoon as I sat down to my breakfast. "I see that you have read it since you have marked it. I don't deny that it is smartly written. It irritates me though. It is evidently the theory of some armchair lounger who evolves all these neat little paradoxes in the **seclusion** of his own study. It is not practical. I should like to see him clapped down in a third-class carriage on the Underground, and asked to give the trades of all his fellow-travellers. I would **lay** a thousand to one against him."

"You would lose your money," Sherlock Holmes remarked calmly. "As for the article, I wrote it myself."

"You!"

turn [tə:rn] n.
소질, 적성
chimerical [kimérikəl, kai-] adj. 황당무계한, 비현실적인, 상상의

"Yes; I have a **turn** both for observation and for deduction. The theories which I have expressed there, and which appear to you to be so **chimerical**, are really extremely practical—so practical that I depend upon them for my bread and cheese."

"And how?" I asked involuntarily.

"Well, I have a trade of my own. I suppose

> misdeed [mìsdíːd] n.
> 나쁜 짓, 비행; 범죄행위
> to have at one's finger's ends:
> 정통한, 잘 아는
> forgery [fɔ́ːrdʒəri] n.
> 위조, 날조, 기만

I am the only one in the world. I'm a consulting detective, if you can understand what that is. Here in London we have lots of Government detectives and lots of private ones. When these fellows are at fault, they come to me, and I manage to put them on the right scent. They lay all the evidence before me, and I am generally able, by the help of my knowledge of the history of crime, to set them straight. There is a strong family resemblance about **misdeeds**, and if you **have** all the details of a thousand **at your finger ends**, it is odd if you can't unravel the thousand and first. Lestrade is a well-known detective. He got himself into a fog recently over a **forgery** case, and that was what brought him here."

"And these other people?"

"They are mostly sent on by private inquiry agencies. They are all people who are in trouble about something and want a little enlightening. I listen to their story, they listen to my comments, and then I pocket my fee."

"But do you mean to say," I said, "that without leaving your room you can unravel some knot which other men can make nothing of, although they have seen every detail for themselves?"

"Quite so. I have a kind of **intuition** that way. Now and again a case turns up which is a little more complex. Then I have to **bustle** about and see things with my own eyes. You see I have a lot of special knowledge which I apply to the problem, and which facilitates matters wonderfully. Those rules of deduction laid down in that article which aroused your scorn, are invaluable to me in practical work. Observation with me is second nature. You appeared to be surprised when I told you, on our first meeting, that you had come from Afghanistan."

"**You were told**, no doubt."

"Nothing of the sort. I *knew* you came from Afghanistan. From long habit the train of thoughts ran so swiftly through my mind, that I arrived at the conclusion without being conscious of intermediate steps. There were such steps, however. The train of reasoning ran, 'Here is a gentleman of a medical type, but with the air of a military man. Clearly an

---

intuition [ìntjuíʃən] n.
직관
bustle [bʌ́sl] v.
분주히 돌아다니다 (움직이다), 서두르다

You were told: You were told by someone that I had come from Afghanistan.
knew: 이탤릭체의 사용은 특정 단어 또는 구를 강조하기 사용됨. 셜록은 "knew"를 발음할 때 액센트를 주거나 잠깐의 휴지를 두어, 이후 기술되는 바와 같이, 본인이 관찰과 분석을 통해 사실을 발견했음을 강조하고 있음

2 The Science of Deduction

> haggard [hǽgərd] adj.
> 수척한, 초췌한
> say [sei] v.
> 나타내다, 가리키다

army doctor, then. He has just come from the tropics, for his face is dark, and that is not the natural tint of his skin, for his wrists are fair. He has undergone hardship and sickness, as his **haggard** face **says** clearly. His left arm has been injured. He holds it in a stiff and unnatural manner. Where in the tropics could an English army doctor have seen much hardship and got his arm wounded? Clearly in Afghanistan.' The whole train of thought did not occupy a second. I then remarked that you came from Afghanistan, and you were astonished."

> "Nothing of the sort. I *knew* you came from Afghanistan..."

"It is simple enough as you explain it," I said, smiling. "You remind me of Edgar Allen Poe's Dupin. I had no idea that such individuals did exist outside of stories."

> compliment [kámpləmənt / kɔ́m-] v.
> 칭찬하다
> apropos [æ̀prəpóu] adj.
> 적절한, 알맞은

Sherlock Holmes rose and lit his pipe. "No doubt you think that you are **complimenting** me in comparing me to Dupin," he observed. "Now, in my opinion, Dupin was a very inferior fellow. That trick of his of breaking in on his friends' thoughts with an **apropos** remark after a quarter of an hour's silence is really very showy and superficial. He had some analytical genius, no doubt; but he was by no means such a phenomenon as Poe appeared to imagine."

"Have you read Gaboriau's works?" I asked. "Does Lecoq come up to your idea of a detective?"

Sherlock Holmes **sniffed sardonically**. "Lecoq was a miserable **bungler**," he said, in an angry voice; "he had only one thing to recommend him, and that was his energy. That book made me positively ill. The question was how to identify an unknown prisoner. I could have done it in twenty-four hours. Lecoq took six months or so. It might be made a text-book for detectives to teach them what to avoid."

I felt rather **indignant** at having two characters whom I had admired treated in this **cavalier** style. I walked over to the window, and stood looking out into the busy street. "This fellow may be very clever," I said to myself, "but he is certainly very **conceited**."

"There are no crimes and no criminals in these days," he said, **querulously**.

---

sniff [snif] v.
경멸하듯 얘기하다
sardonical [sɑːrdánikəl/-dɔ́nikəl] adj.
빈정대는, 야유하는
bungle [bʌ́ŋɡəl] v.
서투르다, 실수하다

indignant [indígnənt] adj.
성난, 화난
cavalier [kæ̀vəlíər] adj.
건방진, 거만한, 호탕한
conceited [kənsíːtid] adj.
자만하는, 으스대는

querulous [kwérjələs] adj.
불평하는, 불만이 많은, 화를 잘 내는

bungling [bʌ́ŋgliŋ] adj.
서투른, 어설픈, 졸렬한
villainy [víləni] n.
악행, 극악함
Scotland Yard:
London Metropolitan
Police force 런던 경찰청

"What is the use of having brains in our profession. I know well that I have it in me to make my name famous. No man lives or has ever lived who has brought the same amount of study and of natural talent to the detection of crime which I have done. And what is the result? There is no crime to detect, or, at most, some **bungling villainy** with a motive so transparent that even a **Scotland Yard** official can see through it."

bumptious [bʌ́mpʃəs] adj.
거만한, 오만한

I was still annoyed at his **bumptious** style of conversation. I thought it best to change the topic.

stalwart [stɔ́:lwə:rt] adj.
건장한, 튼튼한

"I wonder what that fellow is looking for?" I asked, pointing to a **stalwart**, plainly-dressed individual who was walking slowly down the other side of the street, looking anxiously at the numbers. He had a large blue envelope in his hand, and was evidently the bearer of a message.

"You mean the retired sergeant of Marines," said Sherlock Holmes.

brag [bræg] n.
허풍, 뽐냄
bounce [bauns] n.
허풍, 허세

"**Brag** and **bounce**!" thought I to myself. "He knows that I cannot verify his guess."

The thought had hardly passed through my mind when the man whom we were watching caught sight of the number on our door, and ran rapidly across the roadway. We heard a loud knock, a deep voice below, and heavy steps ascending the stair.

"For Mr. Sherlock Holmes," he said, stepping into the room and handing my friend the letter.

Here was an opportunity of taking the conceit out of him. He little thought of

Here was an opportunity of taking the conceit out of him. He little thought of this when he made that random shot.

this when he made that random shot.

"May I ask, my lad," I said, in the blandest voice, "what your trade may be?"

"Commissionaire, sir," he said, **gruffly**. "Uniform away for repairs."

"And you were?" I asked, with a slightly **malicious** glance at my companion.

"A sergeant, sir, Royal Marine Light Infantry, sir. No answer? Right, sir."

He clicked his heels together, raised his hand in a salute, and was gone.

---

gruff [grʌf] adj.
거친, 걸걸한
malicious [məlíʃəs] adj.
악의적인, 심술궂은

3 The Lauriston Garden Mystery

lurk [lə:rk] v.
숨어 기다리다, 잠복하다
dazzle [dǽzəl] v.
혼란시키다, 판단을 흐리게 하다
take in:
속이다, 기만하다
lackluster [lǽklʌ̀stə:r] adj.
흐리멍덩한, 광택이 없는

I confess that I was considerably startled by this fresh proof of the practical nature of my companion's theories. My respect for his powers of analysis increased wondrously. There still remained some **lurking** suspicion in my mind, however, that the whole thing was a prearranged episode, intended to **dazzle** me, though what earthly object he could have in **taking** me **in** was past my comprehension. When I looked at him, he had finished reading the note, and his eyes had assumed the vacant, **lacklustre** expression which

3 The Lauriston Garden Mystery

deduce [didjú:s] v.
추론하다, 추리하다

petulant [pétʃələnt] adj.
언짢은, 초조해하는

brusque [brʌsk / brusk] adj.
무뚝뚝한, 퉁명스러운

smack [smæk] v.
느낌이 나다, 기미가 있다, 맛이 나다

carriage [kǽridʒ] n.
몸가짐, 태도

showed mental abstraction.

"How in the world did you **deduce** that?" I asked.

"Deduce what?" said he, **petulantly**.

"Why, that he was a retired sergeant of Marines."

"I have no time for trifles," he answered, **brusquely**; then with a smile, "Excuse my rudeness. You broke the thread of my thoughts; but perhaps it is as well. So you actually were not able to see that that man was a sergeant of Marines?"

"No, indeed."

"It was easier to know it than to explain why I know it. If you were asked to prove that two and two made four, you might find some difficulty, and yet you are quite sure of the fact. Even across the street I could see a great blue anchor tattooed on the back of the fellow's hand. That **smacked** of the sea. He had a military **carriage**, however, and regulation side whiskers. There we have the marine. He was a man with some amount of self-importance and a certain air of command. You must have observed the way in which he held his head and swung his cane. A steady, respectable, middle-aged man, too, on the face of him—all facts which led me to believe that he had been a sergeant."

"Wonderful!" I **ejaculated**.

"Commonplace," said Holmes, though I thought from his expression that he was pleased at my evident surprise and admiration. "I said just now that there were no criminals. It appears that I am wrong—look at this!" He threw me over the note which the commissionaire had brought.

"Why," I cried, as I cast my eye over it, "this is terrible!"

"It does seem to be a little out of the common," he remarked, calmly. "Would you mind reading it to me aloud?"

This is the letter which I read to him,——

"My Dear Mr. Sherlock Holmes:

"There has been a bad business during the night at 3, Lauriston Gardens, off the Brixton Road. Our man **on the beat** saw a light there about two in the morning, and as the house was an empty one, suspected that something

---

ejaculate [idʒǽkjəlèit] v. (갑자기) 소리치다, 외치다

on the beat: 순찰 중에

was **amiss**. He found the door open, and in the front room, which is **bare** of furniture, discovered the body of a gentleman, well dressed, and having cards in his pocket bearing the name of 'Enoch J. Drebber, Cleveland, Ohio, U.S.A.' There had been no robbery, nor is there any evidence **as to** how the man met his death. There are marks of blood in the room, but there is no wound upon his person. We are **at a loss** as to how he came into the empty house; indeed, the whole affair is a puzzler. If you can come round to the house any time before twelve, you will find me there. I have left everything **in statu quo** until I hear from you. If you are unable to come, I shall give you fuller details, and would **esteem** it a great kindness if you would favour me with your opinion.

"Yours faithfully,

"TOBIAS GREGSON."

"Gregson is the smartest of the Scotland Yarders," my friend remarked; "he and Lestrade are the pick of a bad lot. They

---

amiss [əmís] adj.
잘못된, 정상이 아닌
bare [bɛər] adj.
(가구 등이) 없는
as to ~: ~에 관하여
at a loss: 난처하여, 당황하여, 어찌할 바를 몰라
in statu quo [in-stéitju:-kwóu, -stǽtʃu:]
(Latin) 그대로, 온전히
esteem [istí:m] v.
생각하다, 평가하다

are both quick and energetic, but conventional—shockingly so. They have their knives into one another, too. They are as jealous as a pair of professional beauties. There will be some fun over this case if they are both put upon the scent."

I was amazed at the calm way in which he rippled on. "Surely there is not a moment to be lost," I cried, "shall I go and order you a cab?"

"I'm not sure about whether I shall go. I am the most incurably lazy devil that ever stood in shoe leather—that is, when the fit is on me, for I can be **spry** enough at times."

"Why, it is just such a chance as you have been longing for."

"My dear fellow, what does it matter to me. Supposing I unravel the whole matter, you may be sure that Gregson, Lestrade, and Co. will pocket all the credit. That comes of being an unofficial personage."

"But he begs you to help him."

"Yes. He knows that I am his superior, and acknowledges it to me; but he would cut his tongue out before he would own

spry [sprai] adj.
활발한, 기운찬

it to any third person. However, we may as well go and have a look. I shall work it out on my own hook. I may have a laugh at them if I have nothing else. Come on!"

He hustled on his overcoat, and bustled about in a way that showed that an energetic fit had **superseded** the **apathetic** one.

"Get your hat," he said.

"You wish me to come?"

"Yes, if you have nothing better to do."

A minute later we were both in a hansom, driving furiously for the Brixton Road.

It was a foggy, cloudy morning, and a dun-coloured veil hung over the housetops, looking like the reflection of the mud-coloured streets beneath. My companion was in the best of spirits, and **prattled** away about Cremona fiddles, and the difference between a Stradivarius and an Amati. As for myself, I was silent, for the dull weather and the melancholy business upon which we were engaged, depressed my spirits.

"You don't seem to give much thought to the matter in hand," I said at last, interrupting Holmes' musical **disquisition**.

capital [kǽpitl] adj.
치명적인, 돌이킬 수 없는
bias [báiəs] v.
편견을 갖게 하다

alight [əláit] v.
내리다

minatory [mínətɔ̀:ri / -təri]
adj. 위협적인
tier [tiə:r] n.
층, 열
save [seiv] prep.
을 제외하고

"It is a capital mistake to theorize before you have all the evidence. It biases the judgment."

"No data yet," he answered. "It is a **capital** mistake to theorize before you have all the evidence. It **biases** the judgment."

"You will have your data soon," I remarked, pointing with my finger; "this is the Brixton Road, and that is the house, if I am not very much mistaken."

"So it is. Stop, driver, stop!" We were still a hundred yards or so from it, but he insisted upon our **alighting**, and we finished our journey upon foot.

Number 3, Lauriston Gardens wore an ill-omened and **minatory** look. It was one of four which stood back some little way from the street, two being occupied and two empty. The latter looked out with three **tiers** of vacant melancholy windows, which were blank and dreary, **save** that here and there a "To Let" card had developed like a cataract upon the bleared panes. A small garden sprinkled over with a scattered eruption of sickly plants separated each of these houses from the street, and was traversed by a narrow pathway, yellowish in colour, and consisting apparently of a mixture of clay and of gravel. The whole place

bound [baund] v.
경계를 이루다
stalwart [stɔ́:lwəːrt] adj.
건장한, 튼튼한
constable [kánstəbl / kʌ́n-]
n. 순경

nonchalance [nɑ̀nʃəlɑ́ːns,
nɑ́nʃ-ələns / nɔ́n-] n.
무관심, 냉담
affectation [æ̀fektéiʃən] n.
가장, 허세
scrutiny [skrúːtəni] n.
조사, 심사
flank [flæŋk] v.
옆에 위치하다
rivet [rívit] v.
집중하다, 열중하다

was very sloppy from the rain which had fallen through the night. The garden was **bounded** by a three-foot brick wall with a fringe of wood rails upon the top, and against this wall was leaning a **stalwart** police **constable**, surrounded by a small knot of loafers, who craned their necks and strained their eyes in the vain hope of catching some glimpse of the proceedings within.

I had imagined that Sherlock Holmes would at once have hurried into the house and plunged into a study of the mystery. Nothing appeared to be further from his intention. With an air of **nonchalance** which, under the circumstances, seemed to me to border upon **affectation**, he lounged up and down the pavement, and gazed vacantly at the ground, the sky, the opposite houses and the line of railings. Having finished his **scrutiny**, he proceeded slowly down the path, or rather down the fringe of grass which **flanked** the path, keeping his eyes **riveted** upon the ground. Twice he stopped, and once I saw him smile, and heard him utter an exclamation of satisfaction. There were many marks of footsteps upon the wet clayey soil, but since the police had been coming and going over it, I was unable to see how my companion could hope to learn anything from it. Still I had had such extraordinary evidence of the quickness of his perceptive faculties, that I had no doubt that he could see a great deal which was hidden from me.

At the door of the house we were met by a tall, white-faced, **flaxen**-haired man, with a notebook in his hand, who rushed forward and wrung my companion's hand with **effusion**. "It is indeed kind of you to come," he said, "I have had everything left untouched."

"Except that!" my friend answered, pointing at the pathway. "If a herd of buffaloes had passed along, there could not be a greater mess. No doubt, however, you had drawn your own conclusions, Gregson, before you permitted this."

"I have had so much to do inside the house," the detective said evasively. "My colleague, Mr. Lestrade, is here. I had relied upon him to look after this."

---

flaxen [flǽksən] adj.
아마색, 담황색
effusion [efjúːʒən] n.
감정, 말 등의 분출

> third party:
> 제삼자, 삼자(三者)

Holmes glanced at me and raised his eyebrows sardonically. "With two such men as yourself and Lestrade upon the ground, there will not be much for a **third party** to find out," he said.

Gregson rubbed his hands in a self-satisfied way. "I think we have done all that can be done," he answered; "it's a queer case though, and I knew your taste for such things."

"You did not come here in a cab?" asked Sherlock Holmes.

"No, sir."

"Nor Lestrade?"

"No, sir."

"Then let us go and look at the room."

> inconsequent [inkán-sikwènt, -kwənt / -kɔ́nsikwənt] adj.
> 비논리적인, 일관성이 없는

With which **inconsequent** remark he strode on into the house followed by Gregson, whose features expressed his astonishment.

A short passage, bare planked and dusty, led to the kitchen and offices. Two doors opened out of it to the left and to the right. One of these had obviously been closed for many weeks. The other belonged to the dining-room, which was the apartment in which the mysterious

blotch [blɑtʃ / blɔtʃ] n.
얼룩, 더러움
mildew [míldjù:] n.
곰팡이
surmount [sərmáunt] v.
~의 위에 놓다, ~의 위에 있다

grim [grim] adj.
무서운, 불쾌한

affair had occurred. Holmes walked in, and I followed him with that subdued feeling at my heart which the presence of death inspires.

It was a large square room, looking all the larger from the absence of all furniture. A vulgar flaring paper adorned the walls, but it was **blotched** in places with **mildew**, and here and there great strips had become detached and hung down, exposing the yellow plaster beneath. Opposite the door was a showy fireplace, **surmounted** by a mantelpiece of imitation white marble. On one corner of this was stuck the stump of a red wax candle. The solitary window was so dirty that the light was hazy and uncertain, giving a dull grey tinge to everything, which was intensified by the thick layer of dust which coated the whole apartment.

All these details I observed afterwards. At present my attention was centred upon the single, **grim**, motionless figure which lay stretched upon the boards, with vacant, sightless eyes staring up at the discoloured ceiling. It was that of a man about forty-three or forty-four years of

> immaculate [imǽkjəlit] adj. 티 하나 없는, 깨끗한
> malignant [məlígnənt] adj. 해로운, 악의에 찬
> contortion [kəntɔ́:rʃən] n. 뒤틀림, 일그러짐
> prognathous [prágnəəəs, prɑgnéi- / prɔgnéi-, prɔ́gnə-] adj. 턱이 튀어나온
> simious/simian [símiən] adj. 원숭이와 닮은
> writhe [raið] v. 몸을 뒤틀다, 몸부림치다
> grimy [gráimi] adj. 더러운

age, middle-sized, broad shouldered, with crisp curling black hair, and a short stubbly beard. He was dressed in a heavy broadcloth frock coat and waistcoat, with light-coloured trousers, and **immaculate** collar and cuffs. A top hat, well brushed and trim, was placed upon the floor beside him. His hands were clenched and his arms thrown abroad, while his lower limbs were interlocked as though his death struggle had been a grievous one. On his rigid face there stood an expression of horror, and as it seemed to me, of hatred, such as I have never seen upon human features. This **malignant** and terrible **contortion**, combined with the low forehead, blunt nose, and **prognathous** jaw gave the dead man a singularly **simious** and ape-like appearance, which was increased by his **writhing**, unnatural posture. I have seen death in many forms, but never has it appeared to me in a more fearsome aspect than in that dark, **grimy** apartment, which looked out upon one of the main arteries of suburban London.

Lestrade, lean and ferret-like as ever, was standing by the doorway, and greeted

chime [tʃaim] v.
장단을 맞추다
gout [gaut] n.
방울, 자국

On his rigid face there stood an expression of horror, and as it seemed to me, of hatred, such as I have never seen upon human features.

my companion and myself.

"This case will make a stir, sir," he remarked. "It beats anything I have seen, and I am no chicken."

"There is no clue?" said Gregson.

"None at all," **chimed** in Lestrade.

Sherlock Holmes approached the body, and, kneeling down, examined it intently. "You are sure that there is no wound?" he asked, pointing to numerous **gouts** and

3 The Lauriston Garden Mystery

splashes of blood which lay all round.

"Positive!" cried both detectives.

"Then, of course, this blood belongs to a second individual—presumably the murderer, if murder has been committed. It reminds me of the circumstances attendant on the death of Van Jansen, in Utrecht, in the year '34. Do you remember the case, Gregson?"

"No, sir."

"Read it up—you really should. **There is nothing new under the sun.** It has all been done before."

As he spoke, his **nimble** fingers were flying here, there, and everywhere, feeling, pressing, unbuttoning, examining, while his eyes wore the same far-away expression which I have already remarked upon. So swiftly was the examination made, that one would hardly have guessed the minuteness with which it was conducted. Finally, he sniffed the dead man's lips, and then glanced at the soles of his patent-leather boots.

"He has not been moved at all?" he asked.

"No more than was necessary for the

---

there is ~:
해 아래에는 새 것이 없나니; 전도서 1:9 The thing that hath been, it is that which shall be; and that which is done is that which shall be done: and there is no new thing under the sun.
nimble [nímbəl] adj.
재빠른, 민첩한

purposes of our examination."

"You can take him to the mortuary now," he said. "There is nothing more to be learned."

Gregson had a stretcher and four men at hand. At his call they entered the room, and the stranger was lifted and carried out. As they raised him, a ring tinkled down and rolled across the floor. Lestrade grabbed it up and stared at it with mystified eyes.

"There's been a woman here," he cried. "It's a woman's wedding-ring."

He held it out, as he spoke, upon the palm of his hand. We all gathered round him and gazed at it. There could be no doubt that that circlet of plain gold had once adorned the finger of a bride.

"This complicates matters," said Gregson. "Heaven knows, they were complicated enough before."

"You're sure it doesn't simplify them?" observed Holmes. "There's nothing to be learned by staring at it. What did you find in his pockets?"

"We have it all here," said Gregson, pointing to a litter of objects upon one

As they raised him, a ring tinkled down and rolled across the floor

of the bottom steps of the stairs. "A gold watch, No. 97163, by Barraud, of London. Gold Albert chain, very heavy and solid. Gold ring, with masonic device. Gold pin—bull-dog's head, with rubies as eyes. Russian leather card-case, with cards of Enoch J. Drebber of Cleveland, corresponding with the E. J. D. upon the linen. No purse, but loose money to the extent of seven pounds thirteen. Pocket edition of Boccaccio's *Decameron*, with name of Joseph Stangerson upon the flyleaf. Two letters—one addressed to E. J. Drebber and one to Joseph Stangerson."

"At what address?"

"American Exchange, Strand—to be left till called for. They are both from the Guion Steamship Company, and refer to the sailing of their boats from Liverpool. It is clear that this unfortunate man was about to return to New York."

"Have you made any inquiries as to this man, Stangerson?"

"I did it at once, sir," said Gregson. "I have had advertisements sent to all the newspapers, and one of my men has gone to the American Exchange, but he has not returned yet."

"Have you sent to Cleveland?"

"We telegraphed this morning."

"How did you word your inquiries?"

"We simply detailed the circumstances, and said that we should be glad of any information which could help us."

"You did not ask for particulars on any point which appeared to you to be crucial?"

"I asked about Stangerson."

"Nothing else? Is there no circumstance on which this whole case appears to hinge? Will you not telegraph again?"

"I have said all I have to say," said Gregson, in an offended voice.

Sherlock Holmes chuckled to himself, and appeared to be about to make some remark, when Lestrade, who had been in the front room while we were holding this conversation in the hall, reappeared upon the scene, rubbing his hands in a **pompous** and self-satisfied manner.

"Mr. Gregson," he said, "I have just made a discovery of the highest importance, and one which would have been **overlooked had I not made** a careful

---

pompous [pámpəs / pɔ́m-] adj. 오만한, 뽐내는

overlook [òuvərlúk] v. 모르고 지나치다, 못 보고 넘어가다
had I not made: if I had not made

examination of the walls."

The little man's eyes sparkled as he spoke, and he was evidently in a state of suppressed **exultation** at having scored a point against his colleague.

"Come here," he said, bustling back into the room, the atmosphere of which felt clearer since the removal of its **ghastly** inmate. "Now, stand there!"

He struck a match on his boot and held it up against the wall.

"Look at that!" he said, triumphantly.

I have remarked that the paper had fallen away in parts. In this particular corner of the room a large piece had peeled off, leaving a yellow square of coarse plastering. Across this bare space there was scrawled in blood-red letters a single word—

RACHE

"What do you think of that?" cried the detective, with the air of a showman exhibiting his show. "This was overlooked because it was in the darkest corner of the room, and no one thought of looking there. The murderer has written it with his or her own blood. See this smear where it has trickled down the wall! That disposes of the idea of suicide anyhow. Why was that corner chosen to write it on? I will tell you. See that candle on the mantelpiece. It was lit at the time, and if it was lit this corner would be the brightest instead of the darkest portion of the wall."

"And what does it mean now that you

Across this bare space there was scrawled in blood-red letters a single word—

RACHE

depreciatory [diprí:ʃiətò:ri / -təri] adj. 깎아내리는, 얕보는, 비하하는	
disturb [distə́:rb] v. 방해하다, 어지럽히다.	

have found it?" asked Gregson in a **depreciatory** voice.

"Mean? Why, it means that the writer was going to put the female name Rachel, but was **disturbed** before he or she had time to finish. You mark my words, when this case comes to be cleared up, you will find that a woman named Rachel has something to do with it. It's all very well for you to laugh, Mr. Sherlock Holmes. You may be very smart and clever, but the old hound is the best, when all is said and done."

ruffle [rʌf-əl] v. 화나게 하다, 짜증나게 하다

"I really beg your pardon!" said my companion, who had **ruffled** the little man's temper by bursting into an explosion of laughter. "You certainly have the credit of being the first of us to find this out, and, as you say, it bears every mark of having been written by the other participant in last night's mystery. I have not had time to examine this room yet, but with your permission I shall do so now."

trot [trɑt / trɔt] v. 빠른 걸음으로 가다

As he spoke, he whipped a tape measure and a large round magnifying glass from his pocket. With these two implements he **trotted** noiselessly about the

engross [engróus] v.
몰두하다
covert [kʌ́vərt, kóu-] n.
은신처
incomprehensible [inkàmprihénsəbəl, inkʌ̀m- / inkɔ̀m-] adj.
이해할 수 없는, 불가해한

room, sometimes stopping, occasionally kneeling, and once lying flat upon his face. So **engrossed** was he with his occupation that he appeared to have forgotten our presence, for he chattered away to himself under his breath the whole time, keeping up a running fire of exclamations, groans, whistles, and little cries suggestive of encouragement and of hope. As I watched him I was irresistibly reminded of a pure-blooded, well-trained foxhound, as it dashes backward and forward through the **covert**, whining in its eagerness, until it comes across the lost scent. For twenty minutes or more he continued his researches, measuring with the most exact care the distance between marks which were entirely invisible to me, and occasionally applying his tape to the walls in an equally **incomprehensible** manner. In one place he gathered up very carefully a little pile of grey dust from the floor, and packed it away in an envelope. Finally, he examined with his glass the word upon the wall, going over every letter of it with the most minute exactness. This done,

3 The Lauriston Garden Mystery

he appeared to be satisfied, for he replaced his tape and his glass in his pocket.

"They say that genius is an infinite capacity for taking pains," he remarked with a smile. "It's a very bad definition, but it does apply to detective work."

Gregson and Lestrade had watched the manoeuvres of their amateur companion with considerable curiosity and some contempt. They evidently failed to appreciate the fact, which I had begun to realize, that Sherlock Holmes's smallest actions were all directed towards some definite and practical end.

"What do you think of it, sir?" they both asked.

"It would be robbing you of the credit of the case if I were to presume to help you," remarked my friend. "You are doing so well now that it would be a pity for anyone to interfere." There was a world of **sarcasm** in his voice as he spoke. "If you will let me know how your investigations go," he continued, "I shall be happy to give you any help I can. In the meantime I should like to speak to the

---

"They say that genius is an infinite capacity for taking pains," he remarked with a smile. "It's a very bad definition, but it does apply to detective work."

sarcasm [sáːrkæz-əm] n. 빈정댐, 비꼼, 풍자

constable [kánstəbl / kán-]
n. 순경

prime [praim] n.
전성기, 장년기
florid [fló(:)rid, flár-] adj.
불그레한

incredulous [inkrédʒələs]
adj. 의심하는, 불신하는, 회의적인

constable who found the body. Can you give me his name and address?"

Lestrade glanced at his notebook. "John Rance," he said. "He is off duty now. You will find him at 46, Audley Court, Kennington Park Gate."

Holmes took a note of the address.

"Come along, Doctor," he said; "we shall go and look him up. I'll tell you one thing which may help you in the case," he continued, turning to the two detectives. "There has been murder done, and the murderer was a man. He was more than six feet high, was in the **prime** of life, had small feet for his height, wore coarse, square-toed boots and smoked a Trichinopoly cigar. He came here with his victim in a four-wheeled cab, which was drawn by a horse with three old shoes and one new one on his off foreleg. In all probability the murderer had a **florid** face, and the finger-nails of his right hand were remarkably long. These are only a few indications, but they may assist you."

Lestrade and Gregson glanced at each other with an **incredulous** smile.

| rache [raxə] |
| (German) 복수 |
| cf) 독일어 발음기호 x는 바흐(Bach)의 ch와 같은 발음이 남 |

"If this man was murdered, how was it done?" asked the former.

"Poison," said Sherlock Holmes curtly, and strode off. "One other thing, Lestrade," he added, turning round at the door: "'**Rache**' is the German for 'revenge;' so don't lose your time looking for Miss Rachel."

| parthian shot [pá:rθiən -] |
| 자리를 떠나면서 던지는 한 마디. |
| 고대 파르티아 기병대가 전투 중에 후퇴하면서 뒤로 돌아 쫓아오는 적군에게 화살을 날리던 전술에서 유래함 |
| open-mouthed [óupən-máuðd, -máuθt] adj. |
| 입을 벌린, 몹시 놀란 |

With which **Parthian shot** he walked away, leaving the two rivals **open mouthed** behind him.

4 What John Rance Had to Tell

whence [hwens] adv.
from where, 어디에서, 어디로부터
hail [heil] v.
불러 세우다, 소리쳐 부르다

It was one o'clock when we left No. 3, Lauriston Gardens. Sherlock Holmes led me to the nearest telegraph office, **whence** he dispatched a long telegram. He then **hailed** a cab, and ordered the driver to take us to the address given us by Lestrade.

"There is nothing like first-hand evidence," he remarked; "as a matter of fact, my mind is entirely made up upon the case, but still we may as well learn all that is to be learned."

"You amaze me, Holmes," said I. "Surely

room [ruːm, rum] n.
여지, 경우, 가능성
rut [rʌt] n.
바퀴 자국, 홈

you are not as sure as you pretend to be of all those particulars which you gave."

"There's no **room** for a mistake," he answered. "The very first thing which I observed on arriving there was that a cab had made two **ruts** with its wheels close to the curb. Now, up to last night, we have had no rain for a week, so that those wheels which left such a deep impression must have been there during the night. There were the marks of the horse's hoofs, too, the outline of one of which was far more clearly cut than that of the other three, showing that that was a new shoe. Since the cab was there after the rain began, and was not there at any time during the morning—I have Gregson's word for that—it follows that it must have been there during the night, and, therefore, that it brought those two individuals to the house."

"That seems simple enough," said I; "but how about the other man's height?"

stride [straid] n.
걸음, 보폭

"Why, the height of a man, in nine cases out of ten, can be told from the length of his **stride**. It is a simple calculation enough, though there is no use my boring you with figures. I had this fellow's stride both on the clay outside and on the dust within. Then I had a way of checking my calculation. When a man writes on a wall, his instinct leads him to write above the level of his own eyes. Now that writing was just over six feet from the ground. It was child's play."

"And his age?" I asked.

"Well, if a man can stride four and a half feet without the smallest effort, he can't be quite in the **sere and yellow**. That was the breadth of a **puddle** on the garden walk which he had evidently walked across. Patent-leather boots had gone round, and Square-toes had hopped over. There is no mystery about it at all. I am simply applying to ordinary life a few of those **precepts** of observation and deduction which I **advocated** in that article. Is there anything else that puzzles you?"

"The finger-nails and the Trichinopoly," I suggested.

"The writing on the wall was done with a man's forefinger dipped in blood. My glass allowed me to observe that the

---

sere and yellow [siər-] adj.
늙은, 시들은
puddle [pʌ́dl] n.
물웅덩이
precept [príːsept] n.
교훈
advocate [ǽdvəkèit] v.
주장하다, 변호하다

4 What John Rance Had to Tell   77

plaster was slightly scratched in doing it, which would not have been the case if the man's nail had been trimmed. I gathered up some scattered ash from the floor. It was dark in colour and flakey—such an ash as is only made by a Trichinopoly. I have made a special study of cigar ashes—in fact, I have written a **monograph** upon the subject. I flatter myself that I can distinguish at a glance the ash of any known brand, either of cigar or of tobacco. It is just in such details that the skilled detective differs from the Gregson and Lestrade type."

"And the florid face?" I asked.

"Ah, that was a more daring shot, though I have no doubt that I was right. You must not ask me that at the present state of the affair."

I passed my hand over my brow. "My head is in a **whirl**," I remarked; "the more one thinks of it the more mysterious it grows. How came these two men—if there were two men—into an empty house? What has become of the cabman who drove them? How could one man compel another to take poison? Where did the

---

monograph [mánəgræf, -grà:f / mɔ́n-] n.
학술논문

whirl [hwə:rl] n.
(정신적) 동요, 혼란

decamp [dikǽmp] v.
떠나다

blood come from? What was the object of the murderer, since robbery had no part in it? How came the woman's ring there? Above all, why should the second man write up the German word RACHE before **decamping**? I confess that I cannot see any possible way of reconciling all these facts."

My companion smiled approvingly.

succinct [səksíŋkt] adj.
간결한
blind [blaind] n.
눈속임, 숨기는 수단
clumsy [klʌ́mzi] adj.
서투른, 어색한, 투박한
ruse [ru:z] n.
책략, 음모
divert [divə́:rt, dai-] v.
전환시키다, 돌리다

"You sum up the difficulties of the situation **succinctly** and well," he said. "There is much that is still obscure, though I have quite made up my mind on the main facts. As to poor Lestrade's discovery, it was simply a **blind** intended to put the police upon a wrong track, by suggesting Socialism and secret societies. It was not done by a German. The A, if you noticed, was printed somewhat after the German fashion. Now, a real German invariably prints in the Latin character, so that we may safely say that this was not written by one, but by a **clumsy** imitator who overdid his part. It was simply a **ruse** to **divert** inquiry into a wrong channel. I'm not going to tell you much more of the case, Doctor. You know a

> conjuror gets no credit when once he has explained his trick; and if I show you too much of my method of working, you will come to the conclusion that I am a very ordinary individual after all."

"I shall never do that," I answered; "you have brought detection as near an **exact science** as it ever will be brought in this world."

My companion flushed up with pleasure at my words, and the earnest way in which I uttered them. I had already observed that he was as sensitive to flattery on the score of his art as any girl could be of her beauty.

"I'll tell you one other thing," he said. "Patent leathers and Square-toes came in the same cab, and they walked down the pathway together as friendly as possible—arm-in-arm, in all probability. When they got inside, they walked up and down the room—or rather, Patent-leathers stood still while Square-toes walked up and down. I could read all that in the dust; and I could read that as he walked he grew more and more excited. That is shown by the increased length of

---

conjuror [kʌ́ndʒərər / kɔ́n-] n.
마법사, 마술사

exact science:
정밀과학 (물리, 화학, 천문학 등)

"It was simply a ruse to divert inquiry into a wrong channel."

surmise [sərmáiz, sɔ́ːrmaiz] n.
추측, 짐작
conjecture [kəndʒéktʃər] n. 추측, 억측

dingy [díndʒi] adj.
더러운, 초라한
dreary [dríəri] adj.
우울한, 황량한

quadrangle [kwádræŋgəl / kwɔ́d-] n.
사각형 안뜰
sordid [sɔ́ːrdid] adj.
더러운, 누추한

his strides. He was talking all the while, and working himself up, no doubt, into a fury. Then the tragedy occurred. I've told you all I know myself now, for the rest is mere **surmise** and **conjecture**. We have a good working basis, however, on which to start. We must hurry up, for I want to go to Halle's concert to hear Norman Neruda this afternoon."

This conversation had occurred while our cab had been threading its way through a long succession of **dingy** streets and **dreary** byways. In the dingiest and dreariest of them our driver suddenly came to a stand. "That's Audley Court in there," he said, pointing to a narrow slit in the line of dead-coloured brick. "You'll find me here when you come back."

Audley Court was not an attractive locality. The narrow passage led us into a **quadrangle** paved with flags and lined by **sordid** dwellings. We picked our way among groups of dirty children, and through lines of discoloured linen, until we came to Number 46, the door of which was decorated with a small slip of brass on which the name Rance was engraved.

irritable [írətəbəl] adj.
성마른, 성급한

slumber [slʌ́mbəːr] n.
잠, 수면

pensive [pénsiv] adj.
생각에 잠긴

On inquiry we found that the constable was in bed, and we were shown into a little front parlour to await his coming.

He appeared presently, looking a little **irritable** at being disturbed in his **slumbers**. "I made my report at the office," he said.

Holmes took a half-sovereign from his pocket and played with it **pensively**. "We thought that we should like to hear

it all from your own lips," he said.

"I shall be most happy to tell you anything I can," the constable answered, with his eyes upon the little golden disc.

"Just let us hear it all in your own way as it occurred."

Rance sat down on the horsehair sofa, and knitted his brows, as though determined not to omit anything in his narrative.

"I'll tell it **ye** from the beginning," he said. "My time is from ten at night to six in the morning. At eleven there was a fight at the 'White Hart'; but **bar that** all was quiet enough **on the beat**. At one o'clock it began to rain, and I met Harry Murcher—him who has the Holland Grove beat—and we stood together at the corner of Henrietta Street a-talkin'. Presently—maybe about two or a little after—I thought I would take a look round and see that all was right down the Brixton Road. It was precious dirty and lonely. **Not a soul** did I meet all the way down, though a cab or two went past me. I was a **strollin**' down, thinkin' between ourselves how uncommon handy a four of gin hot would be, when suddenly the **glint** of a

---

ye [ji:,ji] pron.
you 당신
bar that: except that
on the beat:
순찰 중에
not a soul: not a person
stroll [stroul] v.
거닐다, 어슬렁거리다, 산책하다
glint [glint] n.
반짝임, 번득임, 기미

light caught my eye in the window of that same house. Now, I knew that them two houses in Lauriston Gardens was empty on account of him that owns them who won't have the drains seen to, though the very last **tenant** what lived in one of them died **o' typhoid fever**. I was knocked all in a heap, therefore, at seeing a light in the window, and I suspected as something was wrong. When I got to the door——"

"You stopped, and then walked back to the garden gate," my companion interrupted. "What did you do that for?"

Rance gave a violent jump, and stared at Sherlock Holmes with the utmost amazement upon his features.

"Why, that's true, sir," he said; "though how you come to know it, Heaven only knows. Ye see, when I got up to the door it was so still and so lonesome, that I thought I'd be none the worse for some one with me. I **ain't afeared** of anything on this side o' the grave; but I thought that maybe it was him that died o' the typhoid inspecting the drains what killed him. The thought gave me a kind o' **turn**, and I walked back to the gate to see if I

---

tenant [ténənt] n.
거주자
o': of
typhoid fever [táifɔid-] n.
장티푸스

ain't: am not
afeared[əfíərd] adj.
두려운
turn [təːrn] n.
순간적 충격 또는 공포

could see Murcher's lantern, but there wasn't no sign of him nor of anyone else."

"There was no one in the street?"

"Not a livin' soul, sir, nor as much as a dog. Then I pulled myself together and went back and pushed the door open. All was quiet inside, so I went into the room where the light was a-burnin'. There was a candle flickerin' on the mantelpiece—a red wax one—and by its light I saw——"

"Yes, I know all that you saw. You walked round the room several times, and you knelt down by the body, and then you walked through and tried the kitchen door, and then——"

John Rance sprang to his feet with a frightened face and suspicion in his eyes. "Where was you hid to see all that?" he cried. "It seems to me that you knows a deal more than you should."

Holmes laughed and threw his card across the table to the constable. "Don't get arresting me for the murder," he said. "I am one of the hounds and not the wolf; Mr. Gregson or Mr. Lestrade will answer for that. Go on, though. What did you do next?"

Rance resumed his seat, without, however, losing his mystified expression. "I went back to the gate and sounded my whistle. That brought Murcher and two more to the spot."

"Was the street empty then?"

"Well, it was, as far as anybody that could be of any good goes."

"What do you mean?"

The constable's features broadened into a grin. "I've seen many a drunk **chap** in my time," he said, "but never anyone so cryin' drunk as that **cove**. He was at the gate when I came out, a-leanin' up agin the railings, and a-singin' at the pitch o' his lungs about Columbine's New-fangled Banner, or some such stuff. He couldn't stand, far less help."

"What sort of a man was he?" asked Sherlock Holmes. John Rance appeared to be somewhat irritated at this **digression**. "He was an uncommon drunk sort o' man," he said. "He'd ha' found hisself in the station if we hadn't been so took up."

"His face—his dress—didn't you notice them?" Holmes broke in impatiently.

"I should think I did notice them, seeing

---

chap [tʃæp] n.
사내, 아이, 친구
cove [kouv] n.
사람, 친구

digression [daigréʃən, di-]
n. 일탈, 주제에서 벗어남

prop [prɑp / prɔp] v.
부축하다

aggrieved [əgríːvd] adj.
감정이 상한
wager [wéidʒəːr] v.
걸다, 내기하다

"... He couldn't stand, far less help."

that I had to **prop** him up—me and Murcher between us. He was a long chap, with a red face, the lower part muffled round——"

"That will do," cried Holmes. "What became of him?"

"We'd enough to do without lookin' after him," the policeman said, in an **aggrieved** voice. "I'll **wager** he found his way home all right."

"How was he dressed?"

4 What John Rance Had to Tell

"A brown overcoat."

"Had he a whip in his hand?"

"A whip—no."

"He must have left it behind," muttered my companion. "You didn't happen to see or hear a cab after that?"

"No."

"There's a half-sovereign for you," my companion said, standing up and taking his hat. "I am afraid, Rance, that you will never rise in the force. That head of yours should be for use as well as ornament. You might have gained your sergeant's stripes last night. The man whom you held in your hands is the man who holds the clue of this mystery, and whom we are seeking. There is no use of arguing about it now; I tell you that it is so. Come along, Doctor."

We started off for the cab together, leaving our informant **incredulous**, but obviously uncomfortable.

"The **blundering** fool," Holmes said, bitterly, as we drove back to our lodgings. "Just to think of his having such an incomparable bit of good luck, and not **taking advantage of** it."

"... That head of yours should be for use as well as ornament. You might have gained your sergeant's stripes last night..."

incredulous [inkrédʒələs] adj. 의심하는, 불신하는, 회의적인

blunder [blʌ́ndər] v. 큰 실수를 하다, 실책을 범하다
take advantage of ~: ~을 최대한 활용하다

be in the dark:
잘 모르겠다
tally [tǽli] v.
부합하다, 일치하다

lay [lei] v.
내기하다, ~에 걸다
jargon [dʒɑ́ːrgɑn / -gɔn]
n. 전문어, 은어
skein [skein] n.
타래, 뒤엉킴, 혼란
splendid [spléndid] adj.
호화로운, 훌륭한

carol [kǽrəl] v.
노래하다

"I **am rather in the dark** still. It is true that the description of this man **tallies** with your idea of the second party in this mystery. But why should he come back to the house after leaving it? That is not the way of criminals."

"The ring, man, the ring: that was what he came back for. If we have no other way of catching him, we can always bait our line with the ring. I shall have him, Doctor—I'll **lay** you two to one that I have him. I must thank you for it all. I might not have gone but for you, and so have missed the finest study I ever came across: a study in scarlet, eh? Why shouldn't we use a little art **jargon**. There's the scarlet thread of murder running through the colourless **skein** of life, and our duty is to unravel it, and isolate it, and expose every inch of it. And now for lunch, and then for Norman Neruda. Her attack and her bowing are **splendid**. What's that little thing of Chopin's she plays so magnificently: Tra-la-la-lira-lira-lay."

Leaning back in the cab, this amateur bloodhound **carolled** away like a lark

meditate [médətèit] v.
숙고하다, 명상하다

while I **meditated** upon the many-sidedness of the human mind.

"... There's the scarlet thread of murder running through the colourless skein of life, and our duty is to unravel it, and isolate it, and expose every inch of it..."

5 Our Advertisement Brings a Visitor

exertion [igzə́:rʃən] n. 격심한 활동
baboon [bæbú:n / bə-] n. 원숭이
countenance [káuntənəns] n. 얼굴 표정, 안색
sinister [sínistə:r] adj. 불길한, 사악한

Our MORNING'S **exertions** had been too much for my weak health, and I was tired out in the afternoon. After Holmes' departure for the concert, I lay down upon the sofa and endeavoured to get a couple of hours' sleep. It was a useless attempt. My mind had been too much excited by all that had occurred, and the strangest fancies and surmises crowded into it. Every time that I closed my eyes I saw before me the distorted, **baboon**-like **countenance** of the murdered man. So **sinister** was the impression which

bespeak [bispíːk] v.
나타내다
malignant [məlígnənt] adj.
해로운, 악의에 찬
depravity [diprǽvəti] n.
타락, 부패

hypothesis [haipάθəsis / -póθ-] n.
가설
antagonist [æntǽgənist] n.
적대자, 경쟁상대

that face had produced upon me that I found it difficult to feel anything but gratitude for him who had removed its owner from the world. If ever human features **bespoke** vice of the most **malignant** type, they were certainly those of Enoch J. Drebber, of Cleveland. Still I recognized that justice must be done, and that the **depravity** of the victim was no condonement in the eyes of the law.

The more I thought of it the more extraordinary did my companion's **hypothesis**, that the man had been poisoned, appear. I remembered how he had sniffed his lips, and had no doubt that he had detected something which had given rise to the idea. Then, again, if not poison, what had caused the man's death, since there was neither wound nor marks of strangulation? But, on the other hand, whose blood was that which lay so thickly upon the floor? There were no signs of a struggle, nor had the victim any weapon with which he might have wounded an **antagonist**. As long as all these questions were unsolved, I felt that sleep would be no easy matter, either for Holmes or myself. His quiet, self-confident manner convinced me that he had already formed a theory which explained all the facts, though what it was I could not for an instant conjecture.

He was very late in returning—so late, that I knew that the concert could not have **detained** him all the time. Dinner was on the table before he appeared.

"It was magnificent," he said, as he took his seat. "Do you remember what Darwin says about music? He claims that the power of producing and appreciating it existed among the human race long before the power of speech was arrived at. Perhaps that is why we are so subtly influenced by it. There are vague memories in our souls of those **misty** centuries when the world was in its childhood."

"That's rather a broad idea," I remarked.

"One's ideas must be as broad as Nature if they are to interpret Nature," he answered. "What's the matter? You're not looking quite yourself. This Brixton Road affair has upset you."

"To tell the truth, it has," I said. "I ought to be more **case-hardened** after my Afghan experiences. I saw my own comrades hacked to pieces at Maiwand without losing my nerve."

"I can understand. There is a mystery about this which stimulates the imagination; where there is no imagination there is no horror. Have you seen the evening paper?"

"No."

"It gives a fairly good account of the affair. It does not mention the fact that when the man was raised up a woman's wedding ring fell upon the floor. **It is just as well** it does not."

"Why?"

"Look at this advertisement," he answered. "I had one sent to every paper this morning immediately after the affair."

He threw the paper across to me and I glanced at the place indicated. It was the first announcement in the "Found" column. "In Brixton Road, this morning," it ran, "a plain gold wedding ring, found in the roadway between the White Hart Tavern and Holland Grove. Apply Dr. Watson, 221B, Baker Street, between eight and nine this evening."

---

it is just as well:
it is a good thing

dunderhead [dʌ́ndərhèd] n. 바보
meddle [médl] v. 참견하다, 간섭하다

accomplice [əkámplis / əkʌ́m-] n. 공범

"Excuse my using your name," he said. "If I used my own, some of these **dunderheads** would recognize it, and want to **meddle** in the affair."

"That is all right," I answered. "But supposing anyone applies, I have no ring."

"Oh yes, you have," said he, handing me one. "This will do very well. It is almost a facsimile."

"And who do you expect will answer this advertisement?"

"Why, the man in the brown coat—our florid friend with the square toes. If he does not come himself, he will send an **accomplice**."

"Would he not consider it as too dangerous?"

"Not at all. If my view of the case is correct, and I have every reason to believe that it is, this man would rather risk anything than lose the ring. According to my notion he dropped it while stooping over Drebber's body, and did not miss it at the time. After leaving the house he discovered his loss and hurried back, but found the police already in possession, owing

allay [əléi] v.
가라앉히다, 줄이다
occur [əkə́:r] v.
문득 생각나다
overjoy [òuvərdʒɔ́i] v.
크게 기뻐하다

to his own folly in leaving the candle burning. He had to pretend to be drunk in order to **allay** the suspicions which might have been aroused by his appearance at the gate. Now put yourself in that man's place. On thinking the matter over, it must have **occurred** to him that it was possible that he had lost the ring in the road after leaving the house. What would he do then? He would eagerly look out for the evening papers in the hope of seeing it among the articles found. His eye, of course, would light upon this. He would be **overjoyed**. Why should he fear a trap? There would be no reason in his eyes why the finding of the ring should be connected with the murder. He would come. He will come. You shall see him within an hour?"

"And then?" I asked.

"Oh, you can leave me to deal with him then. Have you any arms?"

"I have my old service revolver and a few cartridges."

"You had better clean it and load it. He will be a desperate man; and though I shall take him unawares, it is as well to be ready for anything."

I went to my bedroom and followed his advice. When I returned with the pistol, the table had been cleared, and Holmes was engaged in his favourite occupation of scraping upon his violin.

"The plot thickens," he said, as I entered; "I have just had an answer to my American telegram. My view of the case is the correct one."

"And that is?——" I asked eagerly.

"My fiddle would be the better for new strings," he remarked. "Put your pistol in your pocket. When the fellow comes, speak to him in an ordinary way. Leave the rest to me. Don't frighten him by looking at him too hard."

"It is eight o'clock now," I said, glancing at my watch.

"Yes. He will probably be here in a few minutes. Open the door slightly. That will do. Now put the key on the inside. Thank you! This is a queer old book I picked up at a stall yesterday—*De Jure inter Gentes*—published in Latin at Liége in the Lowlands, in 1642. Charles' head was still firm on his shoulders when this little brown-backed volume was struck off."

"Who is the printer?"

"Philippe de Croy, whoever he may have been. On the **flyleaf**, in very faded ink, is written 'Ex libris Guliolmi Whyte.' I wonder who William Whyte was. Some pragmatical seventeenth-century lawyer, I suppose. His writing has a legal twist about it. Here comes our man, I think."

As he spoke there was a sharp ring at the bell. Sherlock Holmes rose softly and moved his chair in the direction of the door. We heard the servant pass along the hall, and the sharp click of the latch as she opened it.

"Does Dr. Watson live here?" asked a clear but rather harsh voice. We could not hear the servant's reply, but the door closed, and someone began to ascend the stairs. The **footfall** was an uncertain and shuffling one. A look of surprise passed over the face of my companion as he listened to it. It came slowly along the passage, and there was a **feeble** tap at the door.

"Come in," I cried.

---

flyleaf [fláilìːf] n.
책의 앞뒤 백지

footfall [fútfɔ̀ːl] n.
발소리
feeble [fíːbəl] adj.
허약한

hobble [hábəl / hɔ́bəl] v.
발을 절다, 절며 걷다
curtsey/curtsy [kə́:rtsi] n.
(여성이) 무릎과 상체를 굽히는 인사
blear [bliər] adj.
흐릿한
fumble [fʌ́mb-əl] v.
더듬다
disconsolate [diskánsəlit / -kɔ́n-] adj.
불행한, 절망적인
keep one's countenance: 평정을 유지하다 (특히 웃음을 참다)

crone [kroun] n.
쭈그렁할멈

At my summons, instead of the man of violence whom we expected, a very old and wrinkled woman **hobbled** into the apartment. She appeared to be dazzled by the sudden blaze of light, and after dropping a **curtsey**, she stood blinking at us with her **bleared** eyes and **fumbling** in her pocket with nervous, shaky fingers. I glanced at my companion, and his face had assumed such a **disconsolate** expression that it was all I could do to **keep my countenance**.

The old **crone** drew out an evening paper, and pointed at our advertisement. "It's this as has brought me, good gentlemen," she said, dropping another curtsey; "a gold wedding ring in the Brixton Road. It belongs to my girl Sally, as was married only this time twelve-month, which her husband is steward aboard a Union boat, and what he'd say if he comes 'ome and found her without her ring is more than I can think, he being short enough at the best o' times, but more especially when he has the drink. If it please you, she went to the circus last night along with——"

"Is that her ring?" I asked.

"The Lord be thanked!" cried the old woman; "Sally will be a glad woman this night. That's the ring."

"And what may your address be?" I inquired, taking up a pencil.

"13, Duncan Street, Houndsditch. A weary way from here."

"The Brixton Road does not lie between any circus and Houndsditch," said Sherlock

I glanced at my companion, and his face had assumed such a disconsolate expression that it was all I could do to keep my countenance

Holmes sharply.

The old woman faced round and looked keenly at him from her little red-rimmed eyes. "The gentleman asked me for *my* address," she said. "Sally lives in lodgings at 3, Mayfield Place, Peckham."

"And your name is——?"

"My name is Sawyer—her's is Dennis, which Tom Dennis married her—and a smart, clean lad, too, as long as he's at sea, and no steward in the company more thought of; but when on shore, what with the women and what with liquor shops——"

"Here is your ring, Mrs. Sawyer," I interrupted, in obedience to a sign from my companion; "it clearly belongs to your daughter, and I am glad to be able to restore it to the rightful owner."

With many **mumbled** blessings and protestations of gratitude the old crone packed it away in her pocket, and shuffled off down the stairs. Sherlock Holmes sprang to his feet the moment that she was gone and rushed into his room. He returned in a few seconds enveloped in an **ulster** and a **cravat**. "I'll follow her," he said, hurriedly; "she must be

mumble [mʌ́mb-əl] v.
중얼거리다
ulster [ʌ́lstər] n.
외투
cravat [krəvǽt] n.
목에 두르는 스카프, 넥타이

an accomplice, and will lead me to him. Wait up for me." The hall door had hardly slammed behind our visitor before Holmes had descended the stair. Looking through the window I could see her walking feebly along the other side, while her pursuer dogged her some little distance behind. "Either his whole theory is incorrect," I thought to myself, "or else he will be led now to the heart of the mystery." There was no need for him to ask me to wait up for him, for I felt that sleep was impossible until I heard the result of his adventure.

It was close upon nine when he set out. I had no idea how long he might be, but I sat **stolidly** puffing at my pipe and skipping over the pages of Henri Murger's ***Vie de Bohème***. Ten o'clock passed, and I heard the footsteps of the maid as she **pattered** off to bed. Eleven, and the more stately tread of the landlady passed my door, bound for the same destination. It was close upon twelve before I heard the sharp sound of his latchkey. The instant he entered I saw by his face that he had not been successful. Amusement and **chagrin** seemed to be struggling for the

---

stolid [stálid / stól-] adj.
무감동한, 둔감한
Vie de Bohème:
Bohemian life
patter [pǽtər] v.
타닥타닥 걷다(달리다)
chagrin [ʃəgrín / ʃǽgrin]
n. 원통함, 분함

chaff [tʃæf / tʃɑːf] v.
놀리다, 농담을 하다

limp [limp] v.
다리를 절다
footsore [fútsɔ̀ːr] adj.
(많이 걸어) 발이 아픈
genuine [dʒénjuin] adj.
진짜의, 거짓없는
perch [pəːrtʃ] v.
높은 곳에 (앉다)서다, 자리잡다

mastery, until the former suddenly carried the day, and he burst into a hearty laugh.

"I wouldn't have the Scotland Yarders know it for the world," he cried, dropping into his chair; "I have **chaffed** them so much that they would never have let me hear the end of it. I can afford to laugh, because I know that I will be even with them in the long run."

"What is it then?" I asked.

"Oh, I don't mind telling a story against myself. That creature had gone a little way when she began to **limp** and show every sign of being **footsore**. Presently she came to a halt, and hailed a four-wheeler which was passing. I managed to be close to her so as to hear the address, but I need not have been so anxious, for she sang it out loud enough to be heard at the other side of the street, 'Drive to 13, Duncan Street, Houndsditch,' she cried. This begins to look **genuine**, I thought, and having seen her safely inside, I **perched** myself behind. That's an art which every detective should be an expert at. Well, away we rattled, and never drew rein until we reached the street in question. I

stroll [stroul] v.
거닐다, 어슬렁거리다, 산책하다
oath [ouθ] n.
모독적인 표현, 저주, 악담

totter [tátəːr / tɔ́təːr] v.
비틀거리다, 비트적거리다

be taken in:
속다, 속임을 당하다
getup [gétʌp] n.
복장, 옷차림

hopped off before we came to the door, and **strolled** down the street in an easy, lounging way. I saw the cab pull up. The driver jumped down, and I saw him open the door and stand expectantly. Nothing came out though. When I reached him he was groping about frantically in the empty cab, and giving vent to the finest assorted collection of **oaths** that ever I listened to. There was no sign or trace of his passenger, and I fear it will be some time before he gets his fare. On inquiring at Number 13 we found that the house belonged to a respectable paperhanger, named Keswick, and that no one of the name either of Sawyer or Dennis had ever been heard of there."

"You don't mean to say," I cried, in amazement, "that that **tottering**, feeble old woman was able to get out of the cab while it was in motion, without either you or the driver seeing her?"

"Old woman be damned!" said Sherlock Holmes, sharply. "We were the old women to **be so taken in**. It must have been a young man, and an active one, too, besides being an incomparable actor. The **get-up**

inimitable [inímitəbəl]
adj. 비길 데 없는, 모방할 수 없는
give someone the slip: 추격 등을 따돌리다
turn in: 잠자리에 들다

injunction [indʒʌ́ŋkʃən]
n. 권고, 충고
smoulder [smóuldə:r] v. 연기를 내다

was **inimitable**. He saw that he was followed, no doubt, and used this means of **giving me the slip**. It shows that the man we are after is not as lonely as I imagined he was, but has friends who are ready to risk something for him. Now, Doctor, you are looking done-up. Take my advice and **turn in**."

I was certainly feeling very weary, so I obeyed his **injunction**. I left Holmes seated in front of the **smouldering** fire, and long into the watches of the night I heard the low melancholy wailings of his violin, and knew that he was still pondering over the strange problem which he had set himself to unravel.

6 Tobias Gregson Shows What He Can Do

term [tə:rm] v.
부르다, 명명하다
retain [ritéin] v.
보유하다, 유지하다
extract [ikstrǽkt] n.
인용, 발췌
bear on/upon ~:
관계되다, 관련이 있다

The papers next day were full of the "Brixton Mystery," as they **termed** it. Each had a long account of the affair, and some had leaders upon it in addition. There was some information in them which was new to me. I still **retain** in my scrapbook numerous clippings and **extracts bearing upon** the case. Here is a condensation of a few of them:—

The *Daily Telegraph* remarked that

refugee [rèfjudʒíː, ⁻⁻] n. 피난자, 망명자, 난민
revolutionist [rèvəlúːʃənist] n. 혁명가, 혁명당원, 혁명론자
infringe [infríndʒ] v. 위반하다, 침해하다
unwritten law: 불문율, 관습법
admonish [ædmániʃ, əd- / -mɔ́n-] v. 충고하다, 권고하다, 타이르다

outrage [áutrèidʒ] n. 난폭, 폭행, 무도한 행위, 침범, 위반
mass [mæs] n. 일반 대중, 서민, 노동자 계급

in the history of crime there had seldom been a tragedy which presented stranger features. The German name of the victim, the absence of all other motive, and the sinister inscription on the wall, all pointed to its perpetration by political **refugees** and revolutionists. The Socialists had many branches in America, and the deceased had, no doubt, **infringed** their **unwritten laws**, and been tracked down by them. After alluding airily to the Vehmgericht, aqua tofana, Carbonari, the Marchioness de Brinvilliers, the Darwinian theory, the principles of Malthus, and the Ratcliff Highway murders, the article concluded by **admonishing** the Government and advocating a closer watch over foreigners in England.

The *Standard* commented upon the fact that lawless **outrages** of the sort usually occurred under a Liberal administration. They arose from the unsettling of the minds of the **masses**, and the consequent weakening of all authority. The deceased was an American gentleman

bid [bid] v.
말하다
adieu [ədjúː] n.
작별, 고별, 하직
avowed [əváud] adj.
자인한, 공언한
throw(shed, cast) light on :
~을 밝히다, 분명히 하다

who had been residing for some weeks in the metropolis. He had stayed at the boardinghouse of Madame Charpentier, in Torquay Terrace, Camberwell. He was accompanied in his travels by his private secretary, Mr. Joseph Stangerson. The two **bade adieu** to their landlady upon Tuesday, the 4th inst., and departed to Euston Station with the **avowed** intention of catching the Liverpool express. They were afterwards seen together upon the platform. Nothing more is known of them until Mr. Drebber's body was, as recorded, discovered in an empty house in the Brixton Road, many miles from Euston. How he came there, or how he met his fate, are questions which are still involved in mystery. Nothing is known of the whereabouts of Stangerson. We are glad to learn that Mr. Lestrade and Mr. Gregson, of Scotland Yard, are both engaged upon the case, and it is confidently anticipated that these well-known officers will speedily **throw light upon** the matter.

despotism [déspətìzəm] n.
전제정치, 독재정치
continental [kɑ̀ntənéntl / kɔ̀n-] adj.
유럽의, 유럽 대륙의
were they not:
if they were not
stringent [stríndʒ-ənt] adj.
엄격한, 엄중한
infringement [infríndʒmənt] n.
위반, 침해

The *Daily News* observed that there was no doubt as to the crime being a political one. The **despotism** and hatred of Liberalism which animated the **Continental** governments had had the effect of driving to our shores a number of men who might have made excellent citizens **were they not** soured by the recollection of all that they had undergone. Among these men there was a **stringent** code of honour, any **infringement** of which was punished by death. Every effort should be made to find the secretary, Stangerson, and to ascertain some particulars of the habits of the deceased. A great step had been gained by the discovery of the address of the house at which he had boarded—a result which was entirely due to the acuteness and energy of Mr. Gregson of Scotland Yard.

Sherlock Holmes and I read these notices over together at breakfast, and they appeared to afford him considerable amusement.

6 Tobias Gregson Shows What He Can Do

"I told you that, whatever happened, Lestrade and Gregson would be sure to score."

"That depends on how it turns out."

"Oh, bless you, it doesn't matter in the least. If the man is caught, it will be **on account of** their exertions; if he escapes, it will be **in spite of** their exertions. It's **heads I win and tails you lose**. Whatever they do, they will have followers. '**Un sot trouve toujours un plus sot qui l'admire.**'"

"What on earth is this?" I cried, for at this moment there came the pattering of many steps in the hall and on the stairs, accompanied by audible expressions of disgust upon the part of our landlady.

"It's the Baker Street division of the detective police force," said my companion, gravely; and as he spoke there rushed into the room half a dozen of the dirtiest and most ragged **street Arabs** that ever I **clapped eyes on**.

"'**Tention!**" cried Holmes, in a sharp tone, and the six dirty little **scoundrels** stood in a line like so many disreputable statuettes. "In future you shall send up

---

on account of:
~ 때문에
in spite of:
~에도 불구하고
heads I win and tails you lose:
동전을 던져서 앞면이 나오면 내가 이기고 뒷면이 나오면 네가 진다는 의미. 어떤 결과가 나와도 나한테 유리한 상황이 됨을 뜻함
Un sot trouve toujours un plus sot qui l'admire:
(French) 바보는 그를 존경하는 더한 바보들을 찾게 마련이다

street Arab: n.
부랑아, 방랑자, 정처 없는 사람
clap eye on~:
우연히 눈에 띄다, 바라보다

'Tention:
attention 차렷
scoundrel [skáundr-əl] n.
부랑아, 악당

Wiggins alone to report, and the rest of you must wait in the street. Have you found it, Wiggins?"

hain't: have not

"No, sir, we **hain't**," said one of the youths.

"I hardly expected you would. You must keep on until you do. Here are your wages." He handed each of them a shilling. "Now, off you go, and come back with a better report next time."

> scamper [skǽmpəːr] v.
> 뛰어다니다, 허둥지둥 달려가다

He waved his hand, and they **scampered** away downstairs like so many rats, and we heard their shrill voices next moment in the street.

"There's more work to be got out of one of those little beggars than out of a dozen of the force," Holmes remarked. "The mere sight of an official-looking person seals men's lips. These youngsters, however, go everywhere and hear everything. They are as sharp as needles, too; all they want is organisation."

"Is it on this Brixton case that you are employing them?" I asked.

> with a vengeance:
> 몹시, 심하게
> beatitude [biːǽtətjùːd] n.
> 무상의 행복, 지복 (至福)

"Yes; there is a point which I wish to ascertain. It is merely a matter of time. Hullo! we are going to hear some news now **with a vengeance**! Here is Gregson coming down the road with **beatitude** written upon every feature of his face. Bound for us, I know. Yes, he is stopping. There he is!"

There was a violent peal at the bell, and in a few seconds the fair-haired detective came up the stairs, three steps at a time, and burst into our sitting-room.

"My dear fellow," he cried, wringing

Holmes' unresponsive hand, "congratulate me! I have made the whole thing as clear as day."

A shade of anxiety seemed to me to cross my companion's expressive face.

"Do you mean that you are on the right track?" he asked.

"The right track! Why, sir, we have the man **under lock and key**."

"And his name is?"

"Arthur Charpentier, sub-lieutenant in Her Majesty's navy," cried Gregson, pompously rubbing his fat hands and inflating his chest.

Sherlock Holmes gave a sigh of relief, and relaxed into a smile.

"Take a seat, and try one of these cigars," he said. "We are anxious to know how you managed it. Will you have some whiskey and water?"

"I don't mind if I do," the detective answered. "The tremendous exertions which I have gone through during the last day or two have **worn me out**. Not so much bodily exertion, you understand, as the strain upon the mind. You will appreciate that, Mr. Sherlock Holmes,

---

under lock and key:
자물쇠를 채워, 투옥되어

"And his name is?"
"Arthur Charpentier, sub-lieutenant in Her Majesty's navy," cried Gregson, pompously rubbing his fat hands and inflating his chest.

wear out: v.
지치게 하다

gratifying [grǽtəfàiiŋ] adj.
흡족한, 유쾌한

complacent [kəmpléisənt] adj. 기뻐하는, 기분 좋은
paroxysm [pǽrəksìzəm] n. 발작, 격발

tickle [tík-əl] v.
간질이다, 기쁘게 하다

antecedent [æ̀ntəsí:dənt] n.
전력, 경력, 내력

for we are both brain-workers."

"You do me too much honour," said Holmes, gravely. "Let us hear how you arrived at this most **gratifying** result."

The detective seated himself in the arm-chair, and puffed **complacently** at his cigar. Then suddenly he slapped his thigh in a **paroxysm** of amusement.

"The fun of it is," he cried, "that that fool Lestrade, who thinks himself so smart, has gone off upon the wrong track altogether. He is after the secretary Stangerson, who had no more to do with the crime than the babe unborn. I have no doubt that he has caught him by this time."

The idea **tickled** Gregson so much that he laughed until he choked.

"And how did you get your clue?"

"Ah, I'll tell you all about it. Of course, Doctor Watson, this is strictly between ourselves. The first difficulty which we had to contend with was the finding of this American's **antecedents**. Some people would have waited until their advertisements were answered, or until parties came forward and volunteered information. That is not Tobias Gregson's way of going to work. You remember the hat beside the dead man?"

"Yes," said Holmes; "by John Underwood and Sons, 129, Camberwell Road."

Gregson looked quite **crestfallen**.

"I had no idea that you noticed that," he said. "Have you been there?"

"No."

"Ha!" cried Gregson, in a **relieved** voice; "you should never neglect a chance, however small it may seem."

"To a great mind, nothing is little," remarked Holmes, **sententiously**.

"Well, I went to Underwood, and asked him if he had sold a hat of that size and description. He looked over his books, and came on it at once. He had sent the hat to a Mr. Drebber, residing at Charpentier's Boarding Establishment, Torquay Terrace. Thus I got at his address."

"Smart—very smart!" murmured Sherlock Holmes.

"I next called upon Madame Charpentier," continued the detective. "I found her very pale and distressed. Her daughter was in the room, too—an uncommonly fine girl she is, too; she was looking red about the

---

crestfallen [krestfɔ́ːlən] adj. 의기소침한

relieve [rilíːv] v. 누그러뜨리다, 완화시키다

sententious [senténʃəs] adj. 설교투의, 독선적인, 경구적인

eyes and her lips **trembled** as I spoke to her. That didn't escape my notice. I began to smell a rat. You know the feeling, Mr. Sherlock Holmes, when you come upon the right scent—a kind of thrill in your nerves. 'Have you heard of the mysterious death of your late boarder Mr. Enoch J. Drebber, of Cleveland?' I asked.

"The mother nodded. She didn't seem able to get out a word. The daughter burst into tears. I felt more than ever that these people knew something of the matter.

"'At what o'clock did Mr. Drebber leave your house for the train?' I asked.

"'At eight o'clock,' she said, **gulping** in her throat to keep down her **agitation**. 'His secretary, Mr. Stangerson, said that there were two trains—one at 9:15 and one at 11. He was to catch the first.'

"'And was that the last which you saw of him?'

"A terrible change came over the woman's face as I asked the question. Her features turned perfectly **livid**. It was some seconds before she could get out the single word 'Yes'—and when it did come it was in a husky unnatural tone.

"There was silence for a moment, and then the daughter spoke in a calm clear voice.

"'No good can ever come of falsehood, mother,' she said. 'Let us be frank with this gentleman. We *did* see Mr. Drebber again.'

"'God forgive you!' cried Madame Charpentier, throwing up her hands and sinking back in her chair. 'You have murdered your brother.'

"'Arthur would rather that we spoke the truth,' the girl answered firmly.

"'You had best tell me all about it now,' I said. 'Half-confidences are worse than none. Besides, you do not know how much we know of it.'

"'On your head be it, Alice!' cried her mother; and then, turning to me, 'I will tell you all, sir. Do not imagine that my agitation **on behalf of** my son arises from any fear **lest** he should have had a hand in this terrible affair. He is **utterly** innocent of it. My **dread** is, however, that in your eyes and in the eyes of others he may appear to be compromised. That, however, is surely impossible. His high character,

antecedent [æ̀ntəsíːdənt] n. 전력, 경력, 내력

make a clean breast of~: 진실을 말하다

his profession, his **antecedents** would all forbid it.'

"'Your best way is to **make a clean breast** of the facts,' I answered. 'Depend upon it, if your son is innocent he will be none the worse.'

"'Perhaps, Alice, you had better leave us together,' she said, and her daughter withdrew. 'Now, sir,' she continued, 'I had no intention of telling you all this, but since my poor daughter has disclosed it I have no alternative. Having once decided to speak, I will tell you all without omitting any particular.'

"'It is your wisest course,' said I.

otherwise [ʌ́ðərwàiz] adj. 다른
coarse [kɔːrs] adj. 거친, 천한, 교양 없는
brutish [brúːtiʃ] adj. 미개한, 야만적인

"'Mr. Drebber has been with us nearly three weeks. He and his secretary, Mr. Stangerson, had been travelling on the Continent. I noticed a Copenhagen label upon each of their trunks, showing that that had been their last stopping place. Stangerson was a quiet, reserved man, but his employer, I am sorry to say, was far **otherwise**. He was **coarse** in his habits and **brutish** in his ways. The very night of his arrival he became very much the worse for drink, and, indeed, after twelve o'clock in the day he could hardly ever be said to be sober. His manners towards the maid-servants were disgustingly free and familiar. Worst of all, he speedily assumed the same attitude towards my daughter, Alice, and spoke to her more than once in a way which, fortunately, she is too innocent to understand. On one occasion he actually seized her in his arms and embraced her—an outrage which caused his own secretary to reproach him for his unmanly conduct.'

"'But why did you stand all this' I asked. 'I suppose that you can **get rid of** your boarders when you wish.'

"Mrs. Charpentier blushed at my **pertinent** question. 'Would to God that I had given him notice on the very day that he came,' she said. 'But it was a sore temptation. They were paying a pound a day each—fourteen pounds a week, and this is the **slack season**. I am a widow, and my boy in the Navy has cost me much. I **grudged** to lose the money. I acted for the best. This last was too much, however, and I gave him notice to leave on account of it. That was the reason of his going.'

---

get rid of:
없애다, 내보내다

pertinent [pə́:rtənənt] adj.
적절한, 타당한

slack season:
비수기

grudge [grʌdʒ] v.
꺼리다, 아까워하다

> ''Well?'
>
> '''My heart grew light when I saw him drive away. My son is on leave just now, but I did not tell him anything of all this, for his temper is violent, and he is passionately fond of his sister. When I closed the door behind them a load seemed to be lifted from my mind. Alas, in less than an hour there was a ring at the bell, and I learned that Mr. Drebber had returned. He was much excited, and evidently the worse for drink. He forced his way into the room, where I was sitting with my daughter, and made some **incoherent** remark about having missed his train. He then turned to Alice, and before my very face, proposed to her that she should fly with him. "You are **of age**," he said, "and there is no law to stop you. I have money enough and to spare. Never mind the old girl here, but come along with me now straight away. You shall live like a princess." Poor Alice was so frightened that she shrunk away from him, but he caught her by the wrist and endeavoured to draw her towards the door. I screamed, and at that moment my son Arthur came

---

incoherent [ìnkouhíərənt, -hér-] adj.
앞뒤가 맞지 않는, 지리멸렬한

of age:
결혼, 술 구매 또는 법적 책임 등이 가능한 나이의

> oath [ouθ] n.
> 모독적인 표현, 저주, 악담
> scuffle [skʌ́f-əl] n.
> 드잡이, 난투
> that fine fellow:
> 반어적 표현, 저 악당이란 의미

into the room. What happened then I do not know. I heard **oaths** and the confused sounds of a **scuffle**. I was too terrified to raise my head. When I did look up I saw Arthur standing in the doorway laughing, with a stick in his hand. "I don't think **that fine fellow** will trouble us again," he said. "I will just go after him and see what he does with himself." With those words he took his hat and started off down the street. The next morning we heard of Mr. Drebber's mysterious death.'

"This statement came from Mrs. Charpentier's lips with many gasps and pauses. At times she spoke so low that I could hardly catch the words. I made shorthand notes of all that she said, however, so that there should be no possibility of a mistake."

> "It's quite exciting," said Sherlock Holmes, with a yawn.:
> 셜록 홈즈의 말과 행동(하품)이 희극적 대조를 이룸. 흥미롭다는 말과 달리 셜록 홈즈는 지루해하고 있음.

"It's quite exciting," said Sherlock Holmes, with a yawn. "What happened next?"

"When Mrs. Charpentier paused," the detective continued, "I saw that the whole case hung upon one point. Fixing her with my eye in a way which I always found effective with women, I asked her at what hour her son returned.

"'I do not know,' she answered.

"'Not know?'

"'No; he has a latchkey, and he let himself in.'

"'After you went to bed?'

"'Yes.'

"'When did you go to bed?'

"'About eleven.'

"'So your son was gone at least two hours?'

"'Yes.'

"'Possibly four or five?'

"'Yes.'

"'What was he doing during that time?'

"'I do not know,' she answered, turning white to her very lips.

"Of course after that there was nothing more to be done. I found out where Lieutenant Charpentier was, took two officers with me, and arrested him. When I touched him on the shoulder and warned him to come quietly with us, he answered us as bold as brass, 'I suppose you are arresting me for being concerned in the death of that **scoundrel** Drebber,' he said. We had said nothing to him about

---

"I was too terrified to raise my head. When I did look up I saw Arthur standing in the doorway laughing, with a stick in his hand"

scoundrel [skáundr-əl] n.
악당, 무뢰한

it, so that his alluding to it had a most suspicious aspect."

"Very," said Holmes.

"He still carried the heavy stick which the mother described him as having with him when he followed Drebber. It was a **stout** oak **cudgel**."

"What is your theory, then?"

"Well, my theory is that he followed Drebber as far as the Brixton Road. When there, a fresh **altercation** arose between them, in the course of which Drebber received a blow from the stick, in the pit of the stomach perhaps, which killed him without leaving any mark. The night was so wet that no one was about, so Charpentier dragged the body of his victim into the empty house. As to the candle, and the blood, and the writing on the wall, and the ring, they may all be so many tricks to throw the police on to the wrong scent."

"Well done!" said Holmes in an encouraging voice. "Really, Gregson, you are **getting along**. We shall make something of you yet."

"I flatter myself that I have managed

it rather neatly," the detective answered, proudly. "The young man volunteered a statement, in which he said that after following Drebber some time, the latter perceived him, and took a cab in order to get away from him. On his way home he met an old **shipmate**, and took a long walk with him. On being asked where this old shipmate lived, he was unable to give any satisfactory reply. I think the whole case fits together uncommonly well. What amuses me is to think of Lestrade, who had started off upon the wrong scent. I am afraid he won't make much of it. Why, **by Jove**, here's the very man himself!"

It was indeed Lestrade, who had ascended the stairs while we were talking, and who now entered the room. The assurance and **jauntiness** which generally marked his **demeanour** and dress were, however, **wanting**. His face was disturbed and troubled, while his clothes were disarranged and untidy. He had evidently come with the intention of consulting with Sherlock Holmes, for on perceiving his colleague he appeared to

fumble [fʌ́mb-əl] v.
더듬다
incomprehensible
[inkɑ̀mprihénsəbəl,
inkɑ̀m- / inkɔ̀m-] adj.
이해할 수 없는, 불가해한

be embarrassed and put out. He stood in the centre of the room, **fumbling** nervously with his hat and uncertain what to do. "This is a most extraordinary case," he said at last—"a most **incomprehensible** affair."

"Ah, you find it so, Mr. Lestrade!" cried Gregson, triumphantly. "I thought you would come to that conclusion. Have you managed to find the secretary, Mr.

"This is a most extraordinary case," he said at last—"a most incomprehensible affair."

Joseph Stangerson?"

"The secretary, Mr. Joseph Stangerson," said Lestrade gravely, "was murdered at Halliday's Private Hotel about six o'clock this morning"

7 Light in the Darkness

momentous [mouméntəs] adj. 중요한
dumfound [dʌmfáund] v. 깜짝 놀라다

The intelligence with which Lestrade greeted us was so **momentous** and so unexpected, that we were all three fairly **dumfounded**. Gregson sprang out of his chair and upset the remainder of his whiskey and water. I stared in silence at Sherlock Holmes, whose lips were compressed and his brows drawn down over his eyes.

"Stangerson too!" he muttered. "The plot thickens."

grumble[grʌ́mbəl] v. 투덜대다, 불평하다

"It was quite thick enough before," **grumbled** Lestrade, taking a chair, "I

council of war:
전략회의

stammer [stǽməːr] v.
말을 더듬다

seem to have dropped into a sort of **council of war**."

"Are you—are you sure of this piece of intelligence?" **stammered** Gregson.

"I have just come from his room," said Lestrade. "I was the first to discover what had occurred."

"We have been hearing Gregson's view of the matter," Holmes observed. "Would you mind letting us know what you have seen and done?"

"I have no objection," Lestrade answered, seating himself. "I freely confess that I was of the opinion that Stangerson was concerned in the death of Drebber. This fresh development has shown me that I was completely mistaken. Full of the one idea, I set myself to find out what had become of the secretary. They had been seen together at Euston Station about half-past eight on the evening of the third. At two in the morning Drebber had been found in the Brixton Road. The question which confronted me was to find out how Stangerson had been employed between 8:30 and the time of the crime, and what had become of him

vicinity [visínəti] n.
근처, 부근

affirmative [əfə́ːrmətiv] n.
긍정, 확언

afterwards. I telegraphed to Liverpool, giving a description of the man, and warning them to keep a watch upon the American boats. I then set to work calling upon all the hotels and lodging-houses in the **vicinity** of Euston. You see, I argued that if Drebber and his companion had become separated, the natural course for the latter would be to put up somewhere in the vicinity for the night, and then to hang about the station again next morning."

"They would be likely to agree on some meeting-place beforehand," remarked Holmes.

"So it proved. I spent the whole of yesterday evening in making inquiries entirely without avail. This morning I began very early, and at eight o'clock I reached Halliday's Private Hotel, in Little George Street. On my inquiry as to whether a Mr. Stangerson was living there, they at once answered me in the **affirmative**.

"'No doubt you are the gentleman whom he was expecting,' they said. 'He has been waiting for a gentleman for two days.'

"'Where is he now?' I asked.

"'He is upstairs in bed. He wished to be called at nine.'

"'I will go up and see him at once,' I said.

"It seemed to me that my sudden appearance might shake his nerves and lead him to say something unguarded. The **boots** volunteered to show me the room: it was on the second floor, and there was a small corridor leading up to it. The boots pointed out the door to me, and was about to go downstairs again when I saw something that made me feel sickish, in spite of my twenty years' experience. From under the door there curled a little red ribbon of blood, which had **meandered** across the passage and formed a little pool along the skirting at the other side. I gave a cry, which brought the boots back. He nearly **fainted** when he saw it. The door was locked on the inside, but we put our shoulders to it, and knocked it in. The window of the room was open, and beside the window, all huddled up, lay the body of a man in his nightdress. He was quite

---

boots:
호텔 등에서 구두 닦는 등의 일을 하던 사람
meander [miǽndəːr] v.
굽이쳐 흐르다
faint [feint] v.
까무러치다, 아찔해지다

presentiment
[prizéntəmənt] n.
예감, 육감

awestruck [ɔ́:strʌk] adj.
두려워진, 외경심이 생긴

assassin [əsǽsin] n.
암살자, 자객

tingle [tíŋɡəl] v.
쑤시다, 따끔거리다

dead, and had been for some time, for his limbs were rigid and cold. When we turned him over, the boots recognized him at once as being the same gentleman who had engaged the room under the name of Joseph Stangerson. The cause of death was a deep stab in the left side, which must have penetrated the heart. And now comes the strangest part of the affair. What do you suppose was above the murdered man?"

I felt a creeping of the flesh, and a **presentiment** of coming horror, even before Sherlock Holmes answered.

"The word RACHE, written in letters of blood," he said.

"That was it," said Lestrade, in an **awe-struck** voice; and we were all silent for a while.

There was something so methodical and so incomprehensible about the deeds of this unknown **assassin**, that it imparted a fresh ghastliness to his crimes. My nerves, which were steady enough on the field of battle, **tingled** as I thought of it.

"The man was seen," continued Lestrade.

> happen to:
> 우연히(어쩌다) ~하다

"A milk boy, passing on his way to the dairy, **happened to** walk down the lane which leads from the mews at the back of the hotel. He noticed that a ladder, which usually lay there, was raised against one of the windows of the second floor, which was wide open. After passing, he looked back and saw a man descend the ladder. He came down so quietly and openly that the boy imagined him to be some carpenter or joiner at work in the hotel. He took no particular notice of him, beyond thinking in his own mind that it was early for him to be at work. He has an impression that the man was tall, had a reddish face, and was dressed in a long, brownish coat. He must have stayed in the room some little time after the murder, for we found blood-stained water in the basin, where he had washed his hands, and marks on the sheets where he had deliberately wiped his knife."

> tally [tǽli] v.
> 부합하다 일치하다
> exultation [èɡzʌltéiʃən, éksʌl-] n.
> 환희, 기쁨

I glanced at Holmes on hearing the description of the murderer which **tallied** so exactly with his own. There was, however, no trace of **exultation** or satisfaction upon his face.

append [əpénd] v.
부가하다, 서명하다

"Did you find nothing in the room which could furnish a clue to the murderer?" he asked.

"Nothing. Stangerson had Drebber's purse in his pocket, but it seems that this was usual, as he did all the paying. There was eighty odd pounds in it, but nothing had been taken. Whatever the motives of these extraordinary crimes, robbery is certainly not one of them. There were no papers or memoranda in the murdered man's pocket, except a single telegram, dated from Cleveland about a month ago, and containing the words, 'J. H. is in Europe.' There was no name **appended** to this message."

"And there was nothing else?" Holmes asked.

"... There were no papers or memoranda in the murdered man's pocket, except a single telegram, dated from Cleveland about a month ago, and containing the words, 'J. H. is in Europe.'..."

"Nothing of any importance. The man's novel, with which he had read himself to sleep, was lying upon the bed, and his pipe was on a chair beside him. There was a glass of water on the table, and on the window-sill a small chip ointment box containing a couple of pills."

Sherlock Holmes sprang from his chair with an exclamation of delight.

> thread [θred] n.
> 실, 맥락
> tangle [tǽŋg-əl] n.
> 얽힘, 혼란

"The last link," he cried, exultantly. "My case is complete."

The two detectives stared at him in amazement.

"I have now in my hands," my companion said, confidently, "all the **threads** which have formed such a **tangle**. There are, of course, details to be filled in, but I am as certain of all the main facts, from the time that Drebber parted from Stangerson at the station, up to the discovery of the body of the latter, as if I had seen them with my own eyes. I will give you a proof of my knowledge. Could you lay your hand upon those pills?"

> be bound to:
> ~을 해야하는, ~할 예정인, ~할 결심인

"I have them," said Lestrade, producing a small white box; "I took them and the purse and the telegram, intending to have them put in a place of safety at the police station. It was the merest chance my taking these pills, for I **am bound to** say that I do not attach any importance to them."

"Give them here," said Holmes. "Now, Doctor," turning to me, "are those ordinary pills?"

They certainly were not. They were

of a pearly grey colour, small, round, and almost transparent against the light. "From their lightness and transparency, I should imagine that they are soluble in water," I remarked.

"Precisely so," answered Holmes. "Now would you mind going down and **fetching** that poor little devil of a terrier which has been bad so long, and which the landlady wanted you to put out of its pain yesterday?"

I went downstairs and carried the dog upstairs in my arms. Its laboured breathing and glazing eye showed that it was not far from its end. Indeed, its snow-white muzzle proclaimed that it had already exceeded the usual term of **canine** existence. I placed it upon a cushion on the rug.

"I will now cut one of these pills in two," said Holmes, and drawing his penknife he suited the action to the word. "One half we return into the box for future purposes. The other half I will place in this wine glass, in which is a teaspoonful of water. You perceive that our friend, the Doctor, is right, and that it readily

---

fetch [fetʃ] v.
가져오다, 데려오다

canine [kéinain, kǽn-] adj.
개의, 개와 관련된

have to do with ~:
~ 관련이 있다

in time:
장차, 조만간

palatable [pǽlətəbəl] adj.
맛있는, 기분 좋은

dissolves."

"This may be very interesting," said Lestrade, in the injured tone of one who suspects that he is being laughed at; "I cannot see, however, what it **has to do with** the death of Mr. Joseph Stangerson."

"Patience, my friend, patience! You will find **in time** that it has everything to do with it. I shall now add a little milk to make the mixture **palatable**, and on

demeanor [dimí:nər] n.
태도, 품행
draught [dræft, drɑ:ft] n.
마시기, 들이켜기

chagrin [ʃəgrín / ʃǽgrin]
n. 원통함, 분함
derisive [diráisiv, -ziv /
-ríziv, -rís-] adj.
비웃는, 조소하는
by no means:
절대 아닌

presenting it to the dog we find that he laps it up readily enough."

As he spoke he turned the contents of the wine glass into a saucer and placed it in front of the terrier, who speedily licked it dry. Sherlock Holmes's earnest **demeanour** had so far convinced us that we all sat in silence, watching the animal intently, and expecting some startling effect. None such appeared, however. The dog continued to lie stretched upon the cushion, breathing in a laboured way, but apparently neither the better nor the worse for its **draught**.

Holmes had taken out his watch, and as minute followed minute without result, an expression of the utmost **chagrin** and disappointment appeared upon his features. He gnawed his lip, drummed his fingers upon the table, and showed every other symptom of acute impatience. So great was his emotion, that I felt sincerely sorry for him, while the two detectives smiled **derisively**, **by no means** displeased at this check which he had met.

"It can't be a coincidence," he cried, at last springing from his chair and pacing

inert [iná:rt] adj.
비활동성의
wretched [rétʃid] adj.
불쌍한, 한심한, 하찮은
convulsive [kənvʌ́lsiv] adj.
경련성인, 발작적인
shiver [ʃívəːr] n.
떪, 몸의 떨림

perspiration
[pə̀ːrspəréiʃən] n.
땀
invariably [invέəriəbli]
adv. 변함없이

wildly up and down the room; "it is impossible that it should be a mere coincidence. The very pills which I suspected in the case of Drebber are actually found after the death of Stangerson. And yet they are **inert**. What can it mean? Surely my whole chain of reasoning cannot have been false. It is impossible! And yet this **wretched** dog is none the worse. Ah, I have it! I have it!" With a perfect shriek of delight he rushed to the box, cut the other pill in two, dissolved it, added milk, and presented it to the terrier. The unfortunate creature's tongue seemed hardly to have been moistened in it before it gave a **convulsive shiver** in every limb, and lay as rigid and lifeless as if it had been struck by lightning.

Sherlock Holmes drew a long breath, and wiped the **perspiration** from his forehead. "I should have more faith," he said; "I ought to know by this time that when a fact appears to be opposed to a long train of deductions, it **invariably** proves to be capable of bearing some other interpretation. Of the two pills in that box, one was of the most deadly

sober [sóubə:r] adj.
냉정한, 분별있는
conjecture [kəndʒéktʃər] n. 추측

supposition [sʌ̀pəzíʃən] n.
가정, 추측
confound [kənfáund, kɑn- / kɔn-] v.
혼동하다
perplex [pərpléks] v.
당황하게 하다, 혼란시키다
obscure [əbskjúər] adj.
분명치 않은, 불명료한

poison, and the other was entirely harmless. I ought to have known that before ever I saw the box at all."

This last statement appeared to me to be so startling, that I could hardly believe that he was in his **sober** senses. There was the dead dog, however, to prove that his **conjecture** had been correct. It seemed to me that the mists in my own mind were gradually clearing away, and I began to have a dim, vague perception of the truth.

"All this seems strange to you," continued Holmes, "because you failed at the beginning of the inquiry to grasp the importance of the single real clue which was presented to you. I had the good fortune to seize upon that, and everything which has occurred since then has served to confirm my original **supposition**, and, indeed, was the logical sequence of it. Hence things which have **perplexed** you and made the case more **obscure** have served to enlighten me and to strengthen my conclusions. It is a mistake to **confound** strangeness with mystery. The most commonplace crime

> unravel [ʌnrǽvəl] v.
> 풀다, 해결하다
> outré [u:tréi] adj.
> (French) 기이한, 이상한
> render [réndə:r] v.
> ~이 되게 하다

> "It is a mistake to confound strangeness with mystery."

is often the most mysterious, because it presents no new or special features from which deductions may be drawn. This murder would have been infinitely more difficult to **unravel** had the body of the victim been simply found lying in the roadway without any of those *outré* and sensational accompaniments which have **rendered** it remarkable. These strange details, far from making the case more difficult, have really had the effect of making it less so."

Mr. Gregson, who had listened to this address with considerable impatience, could contain himself no longer. "Look here, Mr. Sherlock Holmes," he said, "we are all ready to acknowledge that you are a smart man, and that you have your own methods of working. We want something more than mere theory and preaching now, though. It is a case of taking the man. I have made my case out, and it seems I was wrong. Young Charpentier could not have been engaged in this second affair. Lestrade went after his man, Stangerson, and it appears that he was wrong too. You have thrown out hints here, and hints there, and seem to know more than we do, but the time has come when we feel that we have a right to ask you straight how much you do know of the business. Can you name the man who did it?"

"I cannot help feeling that Gregson is right, sir," remarked Lestrade. "We have both tried, and we have both failed. You have remarked more than once since I have been in the room that you had all the evidence which you require. Surely you will not **withhold** it any longer."

"Any delay in arresting the assassin," I observed, "might give him time to **perpetrate** some fresh **atrocity**."

Thus pressed by us all, Holmes showed signs of **irresolution**. He continued to walk up and down the room with his head sunk on his chest and his brows drawn down, as was his habit when lost in thought.

"There will be no more murders," he said at last, stopping abruptly and facing us. "You can put that consideration out of the question. You have asked me if I know the name of the assassin. I do. The

---

withhold [wiðhóuld, wiθ-]
v. 보류하다, 억누르다

perpetrate [pə́:rpətrèit] v.
범하다, 저지르다
atrocity [ətrásəti / ətrɔ́s-]
n. 극악무도한 짓
irresolution[irèzəlú:ʃən]
n. 우유부단, 망설임

shrewd [ʃru:d] adj.
날카로운, 영리한
desperate [déspərit] adj.
자포자기의, 필사적인
incur [inkə́:r] v.
(좋지 않은 결과에) 빠지다,
(손해 등을) 초래하다

mere knowing of his name is a small thing, however, compared with the power of laying our hands upon him. This I expect very shortly to do. I have good hopes of managing it through my own arrangements; but it is a thing which needs delicate handling, for we have a **shrewd** and **desperate** man to deal with, who is supported, as I have had occasion to prove, by another who is as clever as himself. As long as this man has no idea that anyone can have a clue there is some chance of securing him; but if he had the slightest suspicion, he would change his name, and vanish in an instant among the four million inhabitants of this great city. Without meaning to hurt either of your feelings, I am bound to say that I consider these men to be more than a match for the official force, and that is why I have not asked your assistance. If I fail, I shall, of course, **incur** all the blame due to this omission; but that I am prepared for. At present I am ready to promise that the instant that I can communicate with you without endangering my own combinations, I shall do so."

depreciate [diprí:ʃièit] v.
경시하다, 얕보다, 평가절하하다
spokesman [spóuksmən] n.
대변인
insignificant [ìnsignífikənt] adj.
하찮은, 시시한
unsavory [ʌnséivəri] adj.
맛없는, 재미없는

forelock [fɔ́:rlɑ̀k / -lɔ̀k] n.
앞머리

Gregson and Lestrade seemed to be far from satisfied by this assurance, or by the **depreciating** allusion to the detective police. The former had flushed up to the roots of his flaxen hair, while the other's beady eyes glistened with curiosity and resentment. Neither of them had time to speak, however, before there was a tap at the door, and the **spokesman** of the street Arabs, young Wiggins, introduced his **insignificant** and **unsavoury** person.

"Please, sir," he said, touching his **forelock**, "I have the cab downstairs."

"Good boy," said Holmes, blandly. "Why don't you introduce this pattern at Scotland Yard?" he continued, taking a pair of steel handcuffs from a drawer. "See how beautifully the spring works. They fasten in an instant."

"The old pattern is good enough," remarked Lestrade, "if we can only find the man to put them on."

"Very good, very good," said Holmes, smiling. "The cabman may as well help me with my boxes. Just ask him to step up, Wiggins."

7 Light in the Darkness   143

I was surprised to find my companion speaking as though he were about to set out on a journey, since he had not said anything to me about it. There was a small portmanteau in the room, and this he pulled out and began to strap. He was busily engaged at it when the cabman entered the room.

"Just give me a help with this buckle, cabman," he said, kneeling over his task, and **never turning his head.**

The fellow came forward with a somewhat **sullen, defiant** air, and put down his hands to assist. At that instant there was a sharp click, the jangling of metal, and Sherlock Holmes sprang to his feet again.

"Gentlemen," he cried, with flashing eyes, "let me introduce you to Mr. Jefferson Hope, the murderer of Enoch Drebber and of Joseph Stangerson."

The whole thing occurred in a moment— so quickly that I had no time to realize it. I have a vivid recollection of that instant, of Holmes's triumphant expression and the ring of his voice, of the cabman's dazed, savage face, as he **glared** at the glittering

---

never turning his head: 강한 부정의 의미를 갖는 "never"를 쓴 이유가 있음 직하다. 홈즈는 마부의 의심을 피하기 위해 그와 눈을 마주치길 원치 않았을 것이다.

sullen [sʌ́lən] adj.
시무룩한, 까다로운
defiant [difáiənt] adj.
반항적인, 시비조의

glare [glɛər] v.
노려보다, 쏘아보다

inarticulate [ìnɑːrtíkjəlit] adj.
분명치 않은
roar [rɔːr] n.
고함, 울부짖음, 아우성, 굉음
wrench [rentʃ] v.
비틀다, 잡아떼다
hurl [həːrl] v.
세게 던지다, 내던지다
staghound [-hàund] n.
사냥개

handcuffs, which had appeared as if by magic upon his wrists. For a second or two we might have been a group of statues. Then, with an **inarticulate roar** of fury, the prisoner **wrenched** himself free from Holmes's grasp, and **hurled** himself through the window. Woodwork and glass gave way before him; but before he got quite through, Gregson, Lestrade, and Holmes sprang upon him like so many **staghounds**. He was

For a second or two we might have been a group of statues. Then, with an inarticulate roar of fury, the prisoner wrenched himself free from Holmes's grasp, and hurled himself through the window.

commence [kəméns] v.
시작하다
epileptic [èpəléptik] adj.
간질의
mangle [mǽŋg-əl] v.
상처를 입다, 엉망이 되다
pinion [pínjən] v.
묶다, 구속하다
pant [pænt] v.
숨을 거칠게 내쉬다, 헐떡이다

dragged back into the room, and then **commenced** a terrific conflict. So powerful and so fierce was he that the four of us were shaken off again and again. He appeared to have the convulsive strength of a man in an **epileptic** fit. His face and hands were terribly **mangled** by his passage through the glass, but loss of blood had no effect in diminishing his resistance. It was not until Lestrade succeeded in getting his hand inside his neckcloth and half-strangling him that we made him realize that his struggles were of no avail; and even then we felt no security until we had **pinioned** his feet as well as his hands. That done, we rose to our feet breathless and **panting**.

"We have his cab," said Sherlock Holmes. "It will serve to take him to Scotland Yard. And now, gentlemen," he continued, with a pleasant smile, "we have reached the end of our little mystery. You are very welcome to put any questions that you like to me now, and there is no danger that I will refuse to answer them."

PART 2

The Country of the Saints

1 On the Great Alkali Plain

arid [ǽrid] adj.
건조한
repulsive [ripʌ́lsiv] adj.
적대적인, 강경한 반대의
desolation [dèsəléiʃən] n.
황무지
grim [grim] adj.
무서운, 불쾌한
gloomy [glú:mi] adj.
어두운, 우울한

In the central portion of the great North American Continent there lies an **arid** and **repulsive** desert, which for many a long year served as a barrier against the advance of civilization. From the Sierra Nevada to Nebraska, and from the Yellowstone River in the north to the Colorado upon the south, is a region of **desolation** and silence. Nor is Nature always in one mood throughout this **grim** district. It comprises snow-capped and lofty mountains, and dark and **gloomy** valleys. There are swift-flowing rivers which

jagged [dʒǽgid] adj.
들쭉날쭉한
canon/canyon [kǽnjən] n.
협곡
saline [séili:n, -lain] adj.
염분을 함유한

scrub [skrʌb] n.
관목숲
buzzard [bʌ́zərd] n.
대머리수리
grizzly [grízli] adj.
반백의, 희끗희끗한
lumber [lʌ́mbər] v.
육중하게 움직이다
ravine [rəví:n] n.
계곡, 협곡
sustenance [sʌ́stənəns] n.
생계수단, 음식물

dreary [dríəri] adj.
우울한, 황량한
chaparral [tʃǽpərǽl, ʃæp-]
n. 수풀, 덤불

dash through **jagged cañons**; and there are enormous plains, which in winter are white with snow, and in summer are grey with the **saline** alkali dust. They all preserve, however, the common characteristics of barrenness, inhospitality, and misery.

There are no inhabitants of this land of despair. A band of Pawnees or of Blackfeet may occasionally traverse it in order to reach other hunting-grounds, but the hardiest of the braves are glad to lose sight of those awesome plains, and to find themselves once more upon their prairies. The coyote skulks among the **scrub**, the **buzzard** flaps heavily through the air, and the clumsy **grizzly** bear **lumbers** through the dark **ravines**, and picks up such **sustenance** as it can amongst the rocks. These are the sole dwellers in the wilderness.

In the whole world there can be no more **dreary** view than that from the northern slope of the Sierra Blanco. As far as the eye can reach stretches the great flat plain-land, all dusted over with patches of alkali, and intersected by clumps of the dwarfish **chaparral** bushes.

1 On the Great Alkali Plain

rugged [rʌ́gid] adj.
울퉁불퉁한
fleck [flek] v.
~에 점점이 있다, 점재(點在)하다
appertain [æ̀pərtéin] v.
귀속하다, 관계하다

rut [rʌt] v.
바퀴자국을 내다
glisten [glísn] v.
번쩍거리다

On the extreme verge of the horizon lie a long chain of mountain peaks, with their **rugged** summits **flecked** with snow. In this great stretch of country there is no sign of life, nor of anything **appertaining** to life. There is no bird in the steel-blue heaven, no movement upon the dull, grey earth—above all, there is absolute silence. Listen as one may, there is no shadow of a sound in all that mighty wilderness; nothing but silence—complete and heart-subduing silence.

It has been said there is nothing appertaining to life upon the broad plain. That is hardly true. Looking down from the Sierra Blanco, one sees a pathway traced out across the desert, which winds away and is lost in the extreme distance. It is **rutted** with wheels and trodden down by the feet of many adventurers. Here and there there are scattered white objects which **glisten** in the sun, and stand out against the dull deposit of alkali. Approach, and examine them! They are bones: some large and coarse, others smaller and more delicate. The former have belonged to oxen, and the latter

caravan [kǽrəvæn] n.
대열, 대상(隊商)

genius [dʒíːnjəs, -niəs] n.
수호신, 신령
haggard [hǽgərd] adj.
수척한, 초췌한
luster [lʌ́stər] n.
광택
wiry [wái-əri] adj.
마르고 강인한
vigorous [vígərəs] adj.
활력 있는, 튼튼한
constitution [kànstət-júːʃən / kɔ̀n-] n.
체격, 체질
gaunt [gɔːnt] adj.
여윈, 수척한
shrivel [ʃríːv-əl] v.
시들다, 줄어들다

to men. For fifteen hundred miles one may trace this ghastly **caravan** route by these scattered remains of those who had fallen by the wayside.

Looking down on this very scene, there stood upon the fourth of May, eighteen hundred and forty-seven, a solitary traveller. His appearance was such that he might have been the very **genius** or demon of the region. An observer would have found it difficult to say whether he was nearer to forty or to sixty. His face was lean and **haggard**, and the brown parchment-like skin was drawn tightly over the projecting bones; his long, brown hair and beard were all flecked and dashed with white; his eyes were sunken in his head, and burned with an unnatural **lustre**; while the hand which grasped his rifle was hardly more fleshy than that of a skeleton. As he stood, he leaned upon his weapon for support; and yet his tall figure and the massive framework of his bones suggested a **wiry** and **vigorous constitution**. His **gaunt** face, however, and his clothes, which hung so baggily over his **shrivelled** limbs, proclaimed what it was

1 On the Great Alkali Plain

senile [síːnail, sén-] adj.
노인의
decrepit [dikrépit] adj.
노쇠한, 낡아빠진
toil [tɔil] v.
힘써 일하다, 힘들게 걷다
ravine [rəvíːn] n.
계곡, 협곡
gleam [gliːm] n.
빛남, 번쩍임
crag [kræg] n.
우뚝 솟은 험한 바위
boulder [bóuldəːr] n.
둥근 돌, 바위

sling [sliŋ] v.
메다, 걸다

that gave him that **senile** and **decrepit** appearance. The man was dying—dying from hunger and from thirst.

He had **toiled** painfully down the **ravine**, and on to this little elevation, in the vain hope of seeing some signs of water. Now the great salt plain stretched before his eyes, and the distant belt of savage mountains, without a sign anywhere of plant or tree, which might indicate the presence of moisture. In all that broad landscape there was no **gleam** of hope. North, and east, and west he looked with wild questioning eyes, and then he realized that his wanderings had come to an end, and that there, on that barren **crag**, he was about to die. "Why not here, as well as in a feather bed, twenty years hence?" he muttered, as he seated himself in the shelter of a **boulder**.

Before sitting down, he had deposited upon the ground his useless rifle, and also a large bundle tied up in a grey shawl, which he had carried **slung** over his right shoulder. It appeared to be somewhat too heavy for his strength, for in lowering it, it came down on the ground with some little violence. Instantly there broke from

> In all that broad landscape there was no gleam of hope.

penitent [pénətənt] adj.
참회하는, 뉘우치는
extricate [ékstrəkèit] v.
구출하다, 해방하다
bespeak [bispí:k] v.
~을 나타내다
wan [wɑn / wɔn] adj.
창백한

tousy [tú:zi, táuzi] adj.
헝클어진

the grey parcel a little moaning cry, and from it there protruded a small, scared face, with very bright brown eyes, and two little speckled dimpled fists.

"You've hurt me!" said a childish voice reproachfully.

"Have I though," the man answered **penitently**, "I didn't go for to do it." As he spoke he unwrapped the grey shawl and **extricated** a pretty little girl of about five years of age, whose dainty shoes and smart pink frock with its little linen apron, all **bespoke** a mother's care. The child was pale and **wan**, but her healthy arms and legs showed that she had suffered less than her companion.

"How is it now?" he answered anxiously, for she was still rubbing the **tousy** golden curls which covered the back of her head.

"Kiss it and make it well," she said, with perfect gravity, showing the injured part up to him. "That's what mother used to do. Where's mother?"

"Mother's gone. I guess you'll see her before long."

"Gone, eh!" said the little girl. "Funny, she didn't say goodbye; she 'most always

1 On the Great Alkali Plain

did if she was just goin' over to auntie's for tea, and now she's been away three days. Say, it's awful dry, **ain't** it? Ain't there no water, nor nothing to eat?"

"No, there ain't nothing, dearie. You'll just need to be patient awhile, and then you'll be all right. Put your head up **ag'in** me like that, and then you'll feel **bullier**. It ain't easy to talk when your lips is like leather, but I guess I'd best let you know how the cards lie. What's that you've got?"

"Pretty things! fine things!" cried the little girl enthusiastically, holding up two **glittering** fragments of **mica**. "When we goes back to home I'll give them to brother Bob."

"You'll see prettier things than them soon," said the man confidently. "You just wait a bit. I was going to tell you though—you remember when we left the river?"

"Oh, yes."

"Well, we **reckoned** we'd strike another river soon, d'ye see. But there was somethin' wrong; compasses, or map, or somethin', and it didn't turn up. Water ran out. Just

---

ain't: is not

ag'in: against
bully [búli] adj.
훌륭한, 멋진

glitter [glítər] v.
빛나다
mica [máikə] n.
운모

reckon [rék-ən] v.
생각하다, 추정하다

grimy [gráimi] adj.
더러운
visage [vízidʒ] n.
얼굴, 표정
fust: first
pinafore [pínəfɔ̀:r] n.
어린이용 앞치마

except a little drop for the likes of you, and—and——"

"And you couldn't wash yourself," interrupted his companion gravely, staring up at his **grimy visage**.

"No, nor drink. And Mr. Bender, he was the **fust** to go, and then Indian Pete, and then Mrs. McGregor, and then Johnny Hones, and then, dearie, your mother."

"Then mother's a deader too," cried the little girl, dropping her face in her **pinafore** and sobbing bitterly. "Yes, they all went except you and me. Then I thought there was some chance of water in this direction, so I heaved you over my shoulder and we tramped it together. It don't seem as though we've improved matters. There's an almighty small chance for us now!"

"Do you mean that we are going to die too?" asked the child, checking her sobs, and raising her tear-stained face.

"I guess that's about the size of it."

gleefully [glí:fəli] adv.
매우 기뻐하는
fright [frait] n.
공포, 두려움

"Why didn't you say so before?" she said, laughing **gleefully**. "You gave me such a **fright**. Why, of course, now as long as we die we'll be with mother again."

"Yes, you will, dearie."

"And you too. I'll tell her how awful good you've been. I'll bet she meets us at the door of heaven with a big pitcher of water, and a lot of buckwheat cakes, hot, and toasted on both sides, like Bob and me was fond of. How long will it be first?"

"I don't know—not very long." The man's eyes were fixed upon the northern horizon. In the blue vault of the heaven there had appeared three little specks which increased in size every moment, so rapidly did they approach. They speedily resolved themselves into three large brown birds, which circled over the heads of the two wanderers, and then settled upon some rocks which overlooked them. They were **buzzards**, the vultures of the west, whose coming is the **forerunner** of death.

"Cocks and hens," cried the little girl gleefully, pointing at their ill-omened forms, and clapping her hands to make them rise. "Say, did God make this country?"

"Of course He did," said her companion, rather startled by this unexpected question.

---

buzzard [bʌ́zərd] n.
대머리수리
forerunner [fɔ́ːrrʌ̀nəːr, -́-] n.
선조, 선구자

"He made the country down in Illinois, and He made the Missouri," the little girl continued. "I guess somebody else made the country in these parts. It's not nearly so well done. They forgot the water and the trees."

"What would ye think of offering up prayer?" the man asked **diffidently**.

"It ain't night yet," she answered.

"It don't matter. It ain't quite regular, but He won't mind that, you bet. You say over them ones that you used to say every night in the wagon when we was on the plains."

"Why don't you say some yourself?" the child asked, with wondering eyes.

"I **disremember** them," he answered. "I hain't said none since I was half the height o' that gun. I guess it's never too late. You say them out, and I'll stand by and come in on the choruses."

"Then you'll need to kneel down, and me too," she said, laying the shawl out for that purpose. "You've got to put your hands up like this. It makes you feel kind of good."

It was a strange sight, had there been

---

diffidently [dífidəntli] adv.
조심스럽게

disremember [dìsrimémbər] v.
기억해내지 못하다

1 On the Great Alkali Plain

prattle [prǽtl] v.
떠들다, 지껄이다
chubby [tʃʌ́bi] adj.
오동통한

anything but the buzzards to see it. Side by side on the narrow shawl knelt the two wanderers, the little **prattling** child and the reckless, hardened adventurer. Her **chubby** face, and his haggard, angular visage were both turned up to the cloudless heaven in heartfelt entreaty to that dread Being with whom they were face to face, while the two voices—the one thin and clear, the other deep and

slumber [slʌ́mbəːr] n.
잠
repose [ripóuz] n.
휴식, 휴양
grizzled [grízld] adj.
반백의, 희끗희끗한
tress [tres] n.
머리털, 땋은 머리

Had the wanderer remained awake~:
If the wanderer had remained awake~

harsh—united in the entreaty for mercy and forgiveness. The prayer finished, they resumed their seat in the shadow of the boulder until the child fell asleep, nestling upon the broad breast of her protector. He watched over her **slumber** for some time, but Nature proved to be too strong for him. For three days and three nights he had allowed himself neither rest nor **repose**. Slowly the eyelids drooped over the tired eyes, and the head sunk lower and lower upon the breast, until the man's **grizzled** beard was mixed with the gold **tresses** of his companion, and both slept the same deep and dreamless slumber.

Had the wanderer remained awake for another half-hour a strange sight would have met his eyes. Far away on the extreme verge of the alkali plain there rose up a little spray of dust, very slight at first, and hardly to be distinguished from the mists of the distance, but gradually growing higher and broader until it formed a solid, well-defined cloud. This cloud continued to increase in size until it became evident that it could only

bison [báisən, -zən] n.
아메리카 들소
graze [greiz] v.
(가축 등이 풀을) 뜯어먹다
prairie [prέəri] n.
대평원
bluff [blʌf] n.
절벽, 벼랑
castaway [kǽstəwèi,
kάːst-] n.
난파자, 표류자
tilt [tilt] n.
(마차, 보트 등의) 포장, 덮개, 차양
apparition [æ̀pəríʃən] n.
유령
straggle [strǽg-əl] v.
벗어나다, 낙오하다
innumerable
[injúːmərəbəl] adj.
무수한, 수많은
nomad [nóumæd] n.
유목민, 방랑자

be raised by a great multitude of moving creatures. In more fertile spots the observer would have come to the conclusion that one of those great herds of **bisons** which **graze** upon the **prairie** land was approaching him. This was obviously impossible in these arid wilds. As the whirl of dust drew nearer to the solitary **bluff** upon which the two **castaways** were reposing, the canvas-covered **tilts** of wagons and the figures of armed horsemen began to show up through the haze, and the **apparition** revealed itself as being a great caravan upon its journey for the West. But what a caravan! When the head of it had reached the base of the mountains, the rear was not yet visible on the horizon. Right across the enormous plain stretched the **straggling** array, wagons and carts, men on horseback, and men on foot. **Innumerable** women who staggered along under burdens, and children who toddled beside the wagons or peeped out from under the white coverings. This was evidently no ordinary party of immigrants, but rather some **nomad** people who had been compelled from stress of

clatter [klǽtər] v.
덜컥거리다
rumble [rʌ́mb-əl] v.
덜커덩거리다
creak [kriːk] v.
삐걱거리다
neigh [nei] v.
(말이) 울다
wayfarer [wéifɛ̀-ərəːr] n.
나그네

somber [sʌ́mbəːr / sɔ́m-] adj. 어두컴컴한
homespun [-spʌ̀n] adj.
손으로 만든, 수제의
halt [hɔːlt] v.
멈추다

circumstances to seek themselves a new country. There rose through the clear air a confused **clattering** and **rumbling** from this great mass of humanity, with the **creaking** of wheels and the **neighing** of horses. Loud as it was, it was not sufficient to rouse the two tired **wayfarers** above them.

At the head of the column there rode a score or more of grave iron-faced men, clad in **sombre homespun** garments and armed with rifles. On reaching the base of the bluff they **halted**, and held a short council among themselves.

"The wells are to the right, my brothers," said one, a hardlipped, clean-shaven man with grizzly hair.

"To the right of the Sierra Blanco—so we shall reach the Rio Grande," said another.

"Fear not for water," cried a third. "He who could draw it from the rocks will not now abandon His chosen people."

"Amen! Amen!" responded the whole party.

They were about to resume their journey when one of the youngest and keenest-eyed uttered an exclamation and pointed up

1 On the Great Alkali Plain

flutter [flʌtəːr] v.
펄럭이다
wisp [wisp] n.
한웅큼, 묶음
rein [rein] v.
고삐로 제어하다, 고삐를 당기다
redskin [ˊskìn] n.
북미 인디언

injun [índʒən] n.
아메리칸 인디언

precipitous [prisípətəs] adj.
깎아지른, 절벽의
dexterity [dekstérəti] n.
솜씨좋음, 손재주 있음
flit [flit] v.
경쾌하게 움직이다

at the rugged crag above them. From its summit there **fluttered** a little **wisp** of pink, showing up hard and bright against the grey rocks behind. At the sight there was a general **reining** up of horses and unslinging of guns, while fresh horsemen came galloping up to reinforce the vanguard. The word "**Redskins**" was on every lip.

"There can't be any number of **Injuns** here," said the elderly man who appeared to be in command. "We have passed the Pawnees, and there are no other tribes until we cross the great mountains."

"Shall I go forward and see, Brother Stangerson," asked one of the band.

"And I," "and I," cried a dozen voices.

"Leave your horses below and we will await you here," the elder answered. In a moment the young fellows had dismounted, fastened their horses, and were ascending the **precipitous** slope which led up to the object which had excited their curiosity. They advanced rapidly and noiselessly, with the confidence and **dexterity** of practised scouts. The watchers from the plain below could see them **flit** from rock to rock

plateau [plætóu / -] n.
고원, 대지
barren [bǽrən] adj.
열매를 맺지 않는, 불모의,
메마른, 쓸모없는
placid [plǽsid] adj.
조용한, 평온한
sinewy [sínjuːi] adj.
건장한
infantile [ínfəntàil, -til]
adj. 어린애 같은
plump [plʌmp] adj.
포동포동한

until their figures stood out against the skyline. The young man who had first given the alarm was leading them. Suddenly his followers saw him throw up his hands, as though overcome with astonishment, and on joining him they were affected in the same way by the sight which met their eyes.

On the little **plateau** which crowned the **barren** hill there stood a single giant boulder, and against this boulder there lay a tall man, long-bearded and hard-featured, but of an excessive thinness. His **placid** face and regular breathing showed that he was fast asleep. Beside him lay a little child, with her round white arms encircling his brown **sinewy** neck, and her golden-haired head resting upon the breast of his velveteen tunic. Her rosy lips were parted, showing the regular line of snow-white teeth within, and a playful smile played over her **infantile** features. Her **plump** little white legs, terminating in white socks and neat shoes with shining buckles, offered a strange contrast to the long shrivelled members of her companion. On the ledge of rock above this strange couple there stood three solemn buzzards, who, at the sight of the new comers, uttered **raucous** screams of disappointment and flapped sullenly away.

The cries of the foul birds awoke the two sleepers, who stared about them in bewilderment. The man staggered to his feet and looked down upon the plain which had been so desolate when sleep had overtaken him, and which was now traversed by this enormous body of men and of beasts. His face assumed an expression of incredulity as he gazed, and he passed his bony hand over his eyes. "This is what they call **delirium**, I guess," he **muttered**. The child stood beside him, holding on to the skirt of his coat, and said nothing, but looked all round her with the wondering, questioning gaze of childhood.

The rescuing party were speedily able to convince the two **castaways** that their appearance was no **delusion**. One of them seized the little girl and hoisted her upon his shoulder, while two others supported her **gaunt** companion, and assisted him towards the wagons.

---

raucous [rɔ́ːkəs] adj.
목쉰 소리의

delirium [dilíriəm] n.
환영, 섬망, 열광
mutter [mʌ́təːr] v.
낮고 불명확한 소리로 말하다, 중얼중얼 말하다

castaway [kǽstəwèi, kάːst-] n.
난파자, 표류자
delusion [dilúːʒən] n.
망상, 착각, 현혹
gaunt [gɔːnt] adj.
여윈, 수척한

un [ən]: pron.
one

defiant [difáiənt] adj.
도전적인
ye [ji:, ji] pron.
you 당신(들)

nigh [nai] adj, adv, prep
near, 가까운
persecute [pə́:rsikjù:t] v.
박해하다, 괴롭히다

jest [dʒest] v.
농담하다
stern [stə:rn] adj.
엄격한, 준엄한

"My name is John Ferrier," the wanderer explained; "me and that little **un** are all that's left o' twenty-one people. The rest is all dead o' thirst and hunger away down in the south."

"Is she your child?" asked someone.

"I guess she is now," the other cried, **defiantly**; "she's mine 'cause I saved her. No man will take her from me. She's Lucy Ferrier from this day on. Who are you, though?" he continued, glancing with curiosity at his stalwart, sunburned rescuers; "there seems to be a powerful lot of **ye**."

"**Nigh** upon ten thousand," said one of the young men; "we are the **persecuted** children of God—the chosen of the Angel Merona."

"I never heard tell on him," said the wanderer. "He appears to have chosen a fair crowd of ye."

"Do not **jest** at that which is sacred," said the other, **sternly**. "We are of those who believe in those sacred writings, drawn in Egyptian letters on plates of beaten gold, which were handed unto the holy Joseph Smith at Palmyra. We have

1 On the Great Alkali Plain 167

come from Nauvoo, in the State of Illinois, where we had founded our temple. We have come to seek a refuge from the violent man and from the godless, even though it be the heart of the desert."

The name of Nauvoo evidently recalled recollections to John Ferrier. "I see," he said, "you are the Mormons."

"We are the Mormons," answered his companions with one voice.

"she's mine 'cause I saved her. No man will take her from me. She's Lucy Ferrier from this day on…"

"And where are you going?"

"We do not know. The hand of God is leading us under the person of our Prophet. You must come before him. He shall say what is to be done with you."

They had reached the base of the hill by this time, and were surrounded by crowds of the pilgrims—pale-faced, meek-looking women; strong, laughing children; and anxious earnest-eyed men. Many were the cries of astonishment and of **commiseration** which arose from them when they perceived the youth of one of the strangers and the **destitution** of the other. Their escort did not **halt**, however, but pushed on, followed by a great crowd of Mormons, until they reached a wagon, which was **conspicuous** for its great size and for the **gaudiness** and smartness of its appearance. Six horses were **yoked** to it, whereas the others were furnished with two, or, at most, four **apiece**. Beside the driver there sat a man who could not have been more than thirty years of age, but whose massive head and resolute expression marked him as a leader. He was reading a brown-backed volume, but

---

commiseration [kəmìzəréiʃən] n. 동정
destitution [déstətjùːʃən] n. 결핍, 결여, 극빈
halt [hɔːlt] v. 멈추다
conspicuous [kənspíkjuəs] adj. 눈에 잘 띄는
gaudiness [gɔ́ːdinis] n. 화려하고 속됨, 번지르르함
yoke [jouk] v. 멍에, 멍에를 메우다
apiece [əpíːs] adv. each, 각자에게

as the crowd approached he laid it aside, and listened attentively to an account of the episode. Then he turned to the two castaways.

"If we take you with us," he said, in **solemn** words, "it can only be as believers in our own creed. We shall have no wolves in our **fold**. Better far that your bones should **bleach** in this wilderness than that you should prove to be that little speck of decay which in time corrupts the whole fruit. Will you come with us on these **terms**?"

"Guess I'll come with you on any terms," said Ferrier, with such emphasis that the grave Elders could not restrain a smile. The leader alone retained his stern, impressive expression.

"Take him, Brother Stangerson," he said, "give him food and drink, and the child likewise. Let it be your task also to teach him our holy creed. We have delayed long enough. Forward! On, on to **Zion**!"

"On, on to Zion!" cried the crowd of Mormons, and the words rippled down the long caravan, passing from mouth

murmur [mə́:rmə:r] n.
속삭임, 중얼거림
waif [weif] n.
떠돌이, 부랑자

to mouth until they died away in a dull **murmur** in the far distance. With a cracking of whips and a creaking of wheels the great wagons got into motion, and soon the whole caravan was winding along once more. The Elder to whose care the two **waifs** had been committed, led them to his wagon, where a meal was already awaiting them.

"You shall remain here," he said. "In a few days you will have recovered from your fatigues. In the meantime, remember that now and for ever you are of our religion. Brigham Young has said it, and he has spoken with the voice of Joseph Smith, which is the voice of God."

2 The Flower of Utah

commemorate
[kəmémərèit] v.
기념하다
privation [praivéiʃən] n.
결핍, 박탈
haven [héivən] n.
안식처
unparalleled [ʌnpǽrəlèld]
adj. 전대미문의, 비길 데
없는
impediment [impédəmənt]
n. 방해, 장애물
tenacity [tənǽsəti] n.
고집, 완고함
stout [staut] adj.
강한, 튼튼한

This is not the place to **commemorate** the trials and **privations** endured by the immigrant Mormons before they came to their final **haven**. From the shores of the Mississippi to the western slopes of the Rocky Mountains they had struggled on with a constancy almost **unparalleled** in history. The savage man, and the savage beast, hunger, thirst, fatigue, and disease—every **impediment** which Nature could place in the way—had all been overcome with Anglo-Saxon **tenacity**. Yet the long journey and the accumulated terrors had shaken the hearts of the **stoutest** among

apportion [əpɔ́ːrʃən] v.
나누다, 배분하다

them. There was not one who did not sink upon his knees in heartfelt prayer when they saw the broad valley of Utah bathed in the sunlight beneath them, and learned from the lips of their leader that this was the promised land, and that these virgin acres were to be theirs for evermore.

Young speedily proved himself to be a skilful administrator as well as a resolute chief. Maps were drawn and charts prepared, in which the future city was sketched out. All around farms were **apportioned** and allotted in proportion to the standing of each individual. The tradesman was put to his trade and the artisan to his calling. In the town streets and squares sprang up as if by magic. In the country there was draining and hedging, planting and clearing, until the next summer saw the whole country golden with the wheat crop. Everything prospered in the strange settlement. Above all, the great temple which they had erected in the centre of the city grew ever taller and larger. From the first blush of dawn until the closing of the twilight, the clatter of the hammer and the rasp

2 The Flower of Utah

of the saw was never absent from the monument which the immigrants erected to Him who had led them safe through many dangers.

The two castaways, John Ferrier and the little girl, who had shared his fortunes and had been adopted as his daughter, accompanied the Mormons to the end of their great **pilgrimage**. Little Lucy Ferrier was borne along pleasantly enough in Elder Stangerson's wagon, a retreat which she shared with the Mormon's three wives and with his son, a **headstrong**, **forward** boy of twelve. Having rallied, with the elasticity of childhood, from the shock caused by her mother's death, she soon became a pet with the women, and reconciled herself to this new life in her moving canvas-covered home. In the meantime Ferrier having recovered from his privations, distinguished himself as a useful guide and an **indefatigable** hunter. So rapidly did he gain the **esteem** of his new companions, that when they reached the end of their wanderings, it was **unanimously** agreed that he should be provided with

---

pilgrimage [pílgrimidʒ]n.
순례
headstrong [-strɔ̀:ŋ, -stràŋ] adj. 완고한
forward [fɔ́:rwəːrd] adj.
주제넘은, 건방진
indefatigable [ìndifǽtigəbəl] adj.
끈기있는
esteem [istí:m] n.
존중, 존경
unanimous [ju:nǽnəməs] adj. 같은 의견인, 만장일치인

as large and as fertile a tract of land as any of the settlers, with the exception of Young himself, and of Stangerson, Kemball, Johnston, and Drebber, who were the four principal Elders.

On the farm thus acquired John Ferrier built himself a substantial log-house, which received so many **additions** in succeeding years that it grew into a roomy villa. He was a man of a practical **turn** of mind, keen in his dealings and skilful with his hands. His iron constitution enabled him to work morning and evening at improving and **tilling** his lands. Hence it came about that his farm and all that belonged to him prospered exceedingly. In three years he was better off than his neighbours, in six he was well-to-do, in nine he was rich, and in twelve there were not half a dozen men in the whole of Salt Lake City who could compare with him. From the great inland sea to the distant Wasatch Mountains there was no name better known than that of John Ferrier.

There was one way and only one in which he offended the susceptibilities

addition [ədíʃən] n.
증축
turn [tə:rn] n.
성향, 기질
till [til] v.
경작하다

2 The Flower of Utah

induce [indjú:s] v.
설득하다, 유발하다
lukewarmness [lú:kwɔ̀:rm-nis] n.
미지근함, 미온적임
incur [inkə́:r] v.
(좋지 않은 결과에) 빠지다, (손해 등을) 초래하다
pine [pain] v.
못내 그리워하다, 초췌해지다
celibate [séləbit, -bèit] adj.
금욕주의, 독신의

of his co-religionists. No argument or persuasion could ever **induce** him to set up a female establishment after the manner of his companions. He never gave reasons for this persistent refusal, but contented himself by resolutely and inflexibly adhering to his determination. There were some who accused him of **lukewarmness** in his adopted religion, and others who put it down to greed of wealth and reluctance to **incur** expense. Others, again, spoke of some early love affair, and of a fair-haired girl who had **pined** away on the shores of the Atlantic. Whatever the reason, Ferrier remained strictly **celibate**. In every other respect he conformed to the religion of the young settlement, and gained the name of being an orthodox and straight-walking man.

undertaking [Àndərtéikiŋ] n. 일, 사업
balsamic [bɔ:lsǽmik, bæl-] adj. 방향성의, 향기로운
ruddy [rʌ́di] adj.
건강한 혈색의

Lucy Ferrier grew up within the log-house, and assisted her adopted father in all his **undertakings**. The keen air of the mountains and the **balsamic** odour of the pine trees took the place of nurse and mother to the young girl. As year succeeded to year she grew taller and stronger, her cheek more **ruddy**, and her

wayfarer [wéifè-ərəːr] n.
나그네
lithe [laið] adj.
유연한

herald [hérəld] v.
보도하다, 포고하다

step more elastic. Many a **wayfarer** upon the high road which ran by Ferrier's farm felt long-forgotten thoughts revive in his mind as he watched her **lithe**, girlish figure tripping through the wheatfields, or met her mounted upon her father's mustang, and managing it with all the ease and grace of a true child of the West. So the bud blossomed into a flower, and the year which saw her father the richest of the farmers left her as fair a specimen of American girlhood as could be found in the whole Pacific slope.

It was not the father, however, who first discovered that the child had developed into the woman. It seldom is in such cases. That mysterious change is too subtle and too gradual to be measured by dates. Least of all does the maiden herself know it until the tone of a voice or the touch of a hand sets her heart thrilling within her, and she learns, with a mixture of pride and of fear, that a new and a larger nature has awoken within her. There are few who cannot recall that day and remember the one little incident which **heralded** the dawn

2 The Flower of Utah

of a new life. In the case of Lucy Ferrier the occasion was serious enough in itself, apart from its future influence on her destiny and that of many besides.

It was a warm June morning, and the Latter Day Saints were as busy as the bees whose **hive** they have chosen for their **emblem**. In the fields and in the streets rose the same **hum** of human industry. Down the dusty high roads **defiled** long streams of heavily laden mules, all heading to the west, for the gold fever had broken out in California, and the overland route lay through the city of the Elect. There, too, were **droves** of sheep and bullocks coming in from the **outlying** pasture lands, and trains of tired immigrants, men and horses equally weary of their **interminable** journey. Through all this **motley** assemblage, threading her way with the skill of an accomplished rider, there galloped Lucy Ferrier, her fair face flushed with the exercise and her long chestnut hair floating out behind her. She had a commission from her father in the city, and was dashing in as she had done many a

---

hive [haiv] n.
벌통
emblem [émbləm] n.
상징, 표상
hum [hʌm] n.
와글거림, 잡음
defile [difáil] v.
일렬로 또는 집단으로 나아가다
drove [drouv] n.
가축떼
outlying [áutlàiiŋ] adj.
외부의, 외딴
interminable [intə́:rmənəbəl] adj.
끝없는
motley [mátli / mɔ́t-] adj.
잡다한, 얼룩덜룩한, 뒤죽박죽의

peltry [péltri] n.
모피
stoicism [stóuəsìz-əm] n.
금욕주의

drove [drouv] n. 가축떼
herdsman [hə́:rdzmən] n.
목동
endeavor [endévər] v.
노력하다, 애쓰다
scarcely [skéə:rsli] adv.
겨우, 가까스로
embed [imbéd] v.
끼워 넣다
cavalcade [kæ̀vəlkéid] n.
행진

time before, with all the fearlessness of youth, thinking only of her task and how it was to be performed. The travel-stained adventurers gazed after her in astonishment, and even the unemotional Indians, journeying in with their **peltries**, relaxed their accustomed **stoicism** as they marvelled at the beauty of the pale-faced maiden.

She had reached the outskirts of the city when she found the road blocked by a great **drove** of cattle, driven by a half-dozen wild-looking **herdsmen** from the plains. In her impatience she **endeavoured** to pass this obstacle by pushing her horse into what appeared to be a gap. **Scarcely** had she got fairly into it, however, before the beasts closed in behind her, and she found herself completely **embedded** in the moving stream of fierce-eyed, long-horned bullocks. Accustomed as she was to deal with cattle, she was not alarmed at her situation, but took advantage of every opportunity to urge her horse on, in the hopes of pushing her way through the **cavalcade**. Unfortunately the horns of one of the

flank [flæŋk] n.
옆구리
prance [præns, prɑːns] v.
뒷발로 뛰어오르다
goad [goud] v.
자극하다, 부추기다
bridle [bráidl] n.
굴레

creatures, either by accident or design, came in violent contact with the **flank** of the mustang, and excited it to madness. In an instant it reared up upon its hind legs with a snort of rage, and **pranced** and tossed in a way that would have unseated any but a skilful rider. The situation was full of peril. Every plunge of the excited horse brought it against the horns again, and **goaded** it to fresh madness. It was all that the girl could do to keep herself in the saddle, yet a slip would mean a terrible death under the hoofs of the unwieldy and terrified animals. Unaccustomed to sudden emergencies, her head began to swim, and her grip upon the **bridle** to relax. Choked by the rising cloud of dust and by the steam from the struggling creatures, she might have abandoned her efforts in despair, but for a kindly voice at her elbow which assured her of assistance. At the same moment a sinewy brown hand caught the frightened horse by the curb, and forcing a way through the drove, soon brought her to the outskirts.

"You're not hurt, I hope, miss," said

her preserver, respectfully.

She looked up at his dark, fierce face, and laughed saucily. "I'm awful frightened," she said, naively; "whoever would have thought that Poncho would have been so scared by a lot of cows?"

"Thank God, you kept your seat," the other said, earnestly. He was a tall, savage-looking young fellow, mounted on a powerful **roan** horse, and clad in the

roan [roun] adj.
붉은색, 검은색 등에 흰털이 섞인

Scarcely had she got fairly into it, however, before the beasts closed in behind her, and she found herself completely embedded in the moving stream of fierce-eyed, long-horned bullocks

rough dress of a hunter, with a long rifle slung over his shoulders. "I guess you are the daughter of John Ferrier," he remarked; "I saw you ride down from his house. When you see him, ask him if he remembers the Jefferson Hopes of St. Louis. If he's the same Ferrier, my father and he were pretty **thick**."

"Hadn't you better come and ask yourself?" she asked, **demurely**.

The young fellow seemed pleased at the suggestion, and his dark eyes sparkled with pleasure. "I'll do so," he said, "we've been in the mountains for two months, and are not over and above in visiting condition. He must take us as he finds us."

"He has a good deal to thank you for, and so have I," she answered, "he's awful fond of me. If those cows had jumped on me he'd have never got over it."

"Neither would I," said her companion.

"You! Well, I don't see that it would make much matter to you, anyhow. You ain't even a friend of ours."

The young hunter's dark face grew so gloomy over this remark that Lucy

---

thick [θik] adj.
친밀한

demure [dimjúər] adj.
조심스러운, 얌전한

Ferrier laughed aloud.

"There, I didn't mean that," she said; "of course, you are a friend now. You must come and see us. Now I must push along, or father won't trust me with his business any more. Good-bye!"

"Good-bye," he answered, raising his broad **sombrero**, and bending over her little hand. She wheeled her mustang round, gave it a cut with her riding-whip, and darted away down the broad road in a rolling cloud of dust.

Young Jefferson Hope rode on with his companions, gloomy and **taciturn**. He and they had been among the Nevada Mountains prospecting for silver, and were returning to Salt Lake City in the hope of raising capital enough to work some **lodes** which they had discovered. He had been as keen as any of them upon the business until this sudden incident had drawn his thoughts into another channel. The sight of the fair young girl, as frank and wholesome as the Sierra breezes, had stirred his volcanic, **untamed** heart to its very depths. When she had vanished from his sight,

2 The Flower of Utah

imperious [impíəriəs] adj.
오만한
perseverance [pə̀:rsəvíːrəns] n.
인내, 버팀
render [réndəːr] v.
~이 되게 하다

cooped up:
~에 틀어박혀 있다
halcyon [hǽlsiən] adj.
평온한, 번영하는

he realized that a crisis had come in his life, and that neither silver speculations nor any other questions could ever be of such importance to him as this new and all-absorbing one. The love which had sprung up in his heart was not the sudden, changeable fancy of a boy, but rather the wild, fierce passion of a man of strong will and **imperious** temper. He had been accustomed to succeed in all that he undertook. He swore in his heart that he would not fail in this if human effort and human **perseverance** could **render** him successful.

He called on John Ferrier that night, and many times again, until his face was a familiar one at the farmhouse. John, **cooped up** in the valley, and absorbed in his work, had had little chance of learning the news of the outside world during the last twelve years. All this Jefferson Hope was able to tell him, and in a style which interested Lucy as well as her father. He had been a pioneer in California, and could narrate many a strange tale of fortunes made and fortunes lost in those wild, **halcyon** days.

He had been a scout too, and a trapper, a silver explorer, and a ranchman. Wherever stirring adventures were to be had, Jefferson Hope had been there in search of them. He soon became a favourite with the old farmer, who spoke eloquently of his virtues. On such occasions, Lucy was silent, but her blushing cheek and her bright, happy eyes showed only too clearly that her young heart was no longer her own. Her honest father may not have observed these symptoms, but they were assuredly not thrown away upon the man who had won her affections.

One summer evening he came galloping down the road and pulled up at the gate. She was at the doorway, and came down to meet him. He threw the bridle over the fence and strode up the pathway.

"I am off, Lucy," he said, taking her two hands in his, and gazing tenderly down into her face; "I won't ask you to come with me now, but will you be ready to come when I am here again?"

"And when will that be?" she asked, blushing and laughing.

"A couple of months **at the outside**. I

at the outside:
기껏해야, 많아야

will come and claim you then, my darling. There's no one who can stand between us."

"And how about father?" she asked.

"He has given his consent, **provided** we get these mines working all right. I have no fear on that **head**."

"Oh, well; of course, if you and father have arranged it all, there's no more to be said," she whispered, with her cheek

against his broad breast.

"Thank God!" he said, hoarsely, stooping and kissing her. "It is settled, then. The longer I stay, the harder it will be to go. They are waiting for me at the cañon. Good-bye, my own darling—good-bye. In two months you shall see me."

He tore himself from her as he spoke, and, flinging himself upon his horse, galloped furiously away, never even looking round, as though afraid that his resolution might fail him if he took one glance at what he was leaving. She stood at the gate, gazing after him until he vanished from her sight. Then she walked back into the house, the happiest girl in all Utah.

3 John Ferrier Talks with the Prophet

impending [impéndiŋ] adj.
임박한, 곧 일어날 듯한

Three weeks had passed since Jefferson Hope and his comrades had departed from Salt Lake City. John Ferrier's heart was sore within him when he thought of the young man's return, and of the **impending** loss of his adopted child. Yet her bright and happy face reconciled him to the arrangement more than any argument could have done. He had always determined, deep down in his resolute heart, that nothing would ever induce him to allow his daughter to wed a Mormon. Such marriage he regarded as

inflexible [infléksəbəl] adj.
확고한, 불굴의
unorthodox
[ʌ̀nɔ́ːrəədɑ̀ks / -dɔ̀ks] adj.
정통이 아닌, 이단의

with bated breath:
숨을 죽이고
lest [lest] conj.
~하지 않게
misconstrue [mìskənstrúː / miskɔ̀nstrúː] n.
잘못 해석하다, 곡해하다
retribution [rètrəbjúːʃ-ən] n. 응보, 보복

omniscient [ɑmníʃənt / ɔm-] adj.
전지의, 박식한
omnipotent [ɑmnípətənt / ɔm-] adj.
전능의

no marriage at all, but as a shame and a disgrace. Whatever he might think of the Mormon doctrines, upon that one point he was **inflexible**. He had to seal his mouth on the subject, however, for to express an **unorthodox** opinion was a dangerous matter in those days in the Land of the Saints.

Yes, a dangerous matter—so dangerous that even the most saintly dared only whisper their religious opinions **with bated breath**, **lest** something which fell from their lips might be **misconstrued**, and bring down a swift **retribution** upon them. The victims of persecution had now turned persecutors on their own account, and persecutors of the most terrible description. Not the Inquisition of Seville, nor the German Vehmgericht, nor the secret societies of Italy, were ever able to put a more formidable machinery in motion than that which cast a cloud over the state of Utah.

Its invisibility, and the mystery which was attached to it, made this organization doubly terrible. It appeared to be **omniscient** and **omnipotent**, and yet was

3 John Ferrier Talks with the Prophet

neither seen nor heard. The man who held out against the Church vanished away, and none knew **whither** he had gone or what had **befallen** him. His wife and his children awaited him at home, but no father ever returned to tell them how he had fared at the hands of his secret judges. A **rash** word or a hasty act was followed by **annihilation**, and yet none knew what the nature might be of this terrible power which was suspended over them. No wonder that men went about in fear and trembling, and that even in the heart of the wilderness they dared not whisper the doubts which oppressed them.

At first this vague and terrible power was exercised only upon the **recalcitrants** who, having embraced the Mormon faith, wished afterwards to **pervert** or to abandon it. Soon, however, it took a wider range. The supply of adult women was running short, and **polygamy** without a female population on which to draw was a barren doctrine indeed. Strange rumours began to be **bandied about**—rumours of murdered immigrants and rifled camps

---

whither [hwíðə:r] adv. conj.
어디로
befall [bifɔ́:l] v.
일어나다
rash [ræʃ] adj.
무모한, 무분별한
annihilation [ənàiəléiʃən] n. 멸망, 소멸

recalcitrant [rikǽlsətr-ənt] n. 저항자, 반항자
pervert [pə:rvə́:rt] v.
빗나가다, 배교하다
polygamy [pəlígəmi] n.
일부다처
bandy about:
소문 등이 퍼지다

belated [biléitid] adj.
길을 가다 날이 저문
flit [flit] v.
휙 움직이다
corroborate [kərábərèit / -rɔ́b-] v.
확실하게 하다
sinister [sínistə:r] adj.
불길한, 사악한
ill-omened [-óumənd] adj.
불길한, 불운한

ruthless [rú:θlis] adj.
무정한, 무자비한
misgiving [misgíviŋ] n.
의혹, 불안

in regions where Indians had never been seen. Fresh women appeared in the harems of the Elders—women who pined and wept, and bore upon their faces the traces of an unextinguishable horror. **Belated** wanderers upon the mountains spoke of gangs of armed men, masked, stealthy, and noiseless, who **flitted** by them in the darkness. These tales and rumours took substance and shape, and were **corroborated** and recorroborated, until they resolved themselves into a definite name. To this day, in the lonely ranches of the West, the name of the Danite Band, or the Avenging Angels, is a **sinister** and an **ill-omened** one.

Fuller knowledge of the organization which produced such terrible results served to increase rather than to lessen the horror which it inspired in the minds of men. None knew who belonged to this **ruthless** society. The names of the participators in the deeds of blood and violence done under the name of religion were kept profoundly secret. The very friend to whom you communicated your **misgivings** as to the Prophet and his mission might be one of those who would come forth at night with fire and sword to **exact** a terrible **reparation**. Hence every man feared his neighbour, and none spoke of the things which were nearest his heart.

One fine morning John Ferrier was about to set out to his wheatfields, when he heard the click of the latch, and, looking through the window, saw a stout, sandy-haired, middle-aged man coming up the pathway. His heart leapt to his mouth, for this was none other than the great Brigham Young himself. Full of **trepidation**—for he knew that such a visit **boded** him little good—Ferrier ran to the door to greet the Mormon chief. The latter, however, received his salutations coldly, and followed him with a stern face into the sitting-room.

"Brother Ferrier," he said, taking a seat, and eyeing the farmer keenly from under his light-coloured eyelashes, "the true believers have been good friends to you. We picked you up when you were starving in the desert, we shared our food with you, led you safe to the Chosen

---

exact [igzǽkt] v.
요구하다, 강요하다
reparation [rèpəréiʃ-ən] n.
보상

trepidation [trèpədéiʃ-ən] n. 전율, 공포
bode [boud] v.
전조가 되다, 징조가 되다

wax [wæks] v.
~이 되다

expostulation
[ikspástʃulèiʃən/ -pɔ́s-] n.
훈계, 반대

A rash word or a hasty act was followed by annihilation, and yet none knew what the nature might be of this terrible power which was suspended over them

Valley, gave you a goodly share of land, and allowed you to **wax** rich under our protection. Is not this so?"

"It is so," answered John Ferrier.

"In return for all this we asked but one condition: that was, that you should embrace the true faith, and conform in every way to its usages. This you promised to do, and this, if common report says truly, you have neglected."

"And how have I neglected it?" asked Ferrier, throwing out his hands in **expostulation**. "Have I not given to the common fund? Have I not attended at the Temple? Have I not——?"

"Where are your wives?" asked Young, looking round him. "Call them in, that I may greet them."

"It is true that I have not married," Ferrier answered. "But women were few, and there were many who had better claims than I. I was not a lonely man: I had my daughter to attend to my wants."

"It is of that daughter that I would speak to you," said the leader of the Mormons. "She has grown to be the flower of Utah, and has found favour in the eyes of many

3 John Ferrier Talks with the Prophet

who are high in the land."

John Ferrier groaned internally.

"There are stories of her which I would **fain** disbelieve—stories that she is sealed to some **Gentile**. This must be the gossip of idle tongues. What is the thirteenth rule in the code of the sainted Joseph Smith? 'Let every maiden of the true faith marry one of the elect; for if she wed a Gentile, she commits a **grievous** sin.' This being so, it is impossible that you, who profess the holy creed, should suffer your daughter to violate it."

John Ferrier made no answer, but he played nervously with his riding-whip.

"Upon this one point your whole faith shall be tested—so it has been decided in the Sacred Council of Four. The girl is young, and we would not have her wed grey hairs, neither would we **deprive** her of all choice. We Elders have many **heifers**, but our children must also be provided. Stangerson has a son, and Drebber has a son, and either of them would gladly welcome your daughter to his house. Let her choose between them. They are young and rich, and of the true

---

fain [fein]: adv.
기꺼이
gentile [ʤéntail] n.
이교도의
grievous [grí:vəs] adj.
심각한, 무거운, 통탄할

deprive [dipráiv] v.
빼앗다
heifer [héfər] n.
젊은 암소

faith. What say you to that?"

Ferrier remained silent for some little time with his brows knitted.

"You will give us time," he said at last. "My daughter is very young—she is **scarce** of an age to marry."

"She shall have a month to choose," said Young, rising from his seat. "At the end of that time she shall give her answer."

He was passing through the door, when he turned with flushed face and flashing eyes. "It were better for you, John Ferrier," he thundered, "that you and she were now lying blanched skeletons upon the Sierra Blanco, than that you should put your weak wills against the orders of the Holy Four!"

With a threatening gesture of his hand, he turned from the door, and Ferrier heard his heavy step **scrunching** along the shingly path.

He was still sitting with his elbows upon his knees, considering how he should **broach** the matter to his daughter, when a soft hand was laid upon his, and looking up, he saw her standing beside him. One glance at her pale, frightened face showed

---

scarce [skɛəːrs] adj.
불충분한

scrunch [skrʌntʃ] v.
자박자박 밟고 가다

broach [broutʃ] v.
얘기하다, 거론하다

3 John Ferrier Talks with the Prophet

him that she had heard what had passed.

"I could not help it," she said, in answer to his look. "His voice rang through the house. Oh, father, father, what shall we do?"

"Don't you scare yourself," he answered, drawing her to him, and passing his broad, rough hand caressingly over her chestnut hair. "We'll fix it up somehow or another. You don't find your fancy kind o' lessening

"At the end of that time she shall give her answer."

for this chap, do you?"

A sob and a squeeze of his hand were her only answer.

"No; of course not. I shouldn't care to hear you say you did. He's a likely lad, and he's a Christian, which is more than these folk here, in spite o' all their praying and preaching. There's a party starting for Nevada to-morrow, and I'll manage to send him a message letting him know the hole we are in. If I know anything o' that young man, he'll be back here with a speed that would whip electro-telegraphs."

Lucy laughed through her tears at her father's description.

"When he comes, he will advise us for the best. But it is for you that I am frightened, dear. One hears—one hears such dreadful stories about those who oppose the Prophet; something terrible always happens to them."

"But we haven't opposed him yet," her father answered. "It will be time to look out for **squalls** when we do. We have a clear month before us; at the end of that, I guess we had best **shin** out of Utah."

---

squall [skwɔːl] n.
소동, 북새통
shin [ʃin] v.
재빨리 이동하다

"Leave Utah!"

"That's about the size of it."

"But the farm?"

"We will raise as much as we can in money, and let the rest go. To tell the truth, Lucy, it isn't the first time I have thought of doing it. I don't care about **knuckling under** to any man, as these folk do to their darned Prophet. I'm a freeborn American, and it's all new to me. Guess I'm too old to learn. If he comes browsing about this farm, he might chance to run up against a charge of **buckshot** travelling in the opposite direction."

"But they won't let us leave," his daughter objected.

"Wait till Jefferson comes, and we'll soon manage that. In the meantime, don't you **fret** yourself, my dearie, and don't get your eyes swelled up, else he'll be walking into me when he sees you. There's nothing to be **afeared** about, and there's no danger at all."

John Ferrier uttered these **consoling** remarks in a very confident tone, but she could not help observing that he paid unusual care to the fastening of the doors that night, and that he carefully cleaned and loaded the rusty old shot-gun which hung upon the wall of his bedroom.

"... I don't care about knuckling under to any man, as these folk do to their darned Prophet..."

4 A Flight for Life

entrust [entrʌ́st] v.
맡기다, 위임하다
imminent [ímənənt] adj.
임박한, 곧 일어날 듯한

On the morning which followed his interview with the Mormon Prophet, John Ferrier went in to Salt Lake City, and having found his acquaintance, who was bound for the Nevada Mountains, he **entrusted** him with his message to Jefferson Hope. In it he told the young man of the **imminent** danger which threatened them, and how necessary it was that he should return. Having done thus he felt easier in his mind, and returned home with a lighter heart.

As he approached his farm, he was surprised to see a horse hitched to each of

bloated [bloutid] adj.
부풀어 오른, 거만한

hymn [him] n.
찬송가

the posts of the gate. Still more surprised was he on entering to find two young men in possession of his sitting-room. One, with a long pale face, was leaning back in the rocking-chair, with his feet cocked up upon the stove. The other, a bull-necked youth with coarse, **bloated** features, was standing in front of the window with his hands in his pockets whistling a popular **hymn**. Both of them nodded to Ferrier as he entered, and the one in the rocking-chair commenced the conversation.

"Maybe you don't know us," he said. "This here is the son of Elder Drebber, and I'm Joseph Stangerson, who travelled with you in the desert when the Lord stretched out His hand and gathered you into the true fold."

nasal [néizəl] adj.
콧소리의

"As He will all the nations in His own good time," said the other in a **nasal** voice; "He grindeth slowly but exceeding small."

John Ferrier bowed coldly. He had guessed who his visitors were.

solicit [səlísit] v.
간청하다

"We have come," continued Stangerson, "at the advice of our fathers to **solicit**

4 A Flight for Life

but : only

nay [nei] n. adv.
no

rejoin [riːdʒɔ́in] v.
대답하다
smirk [sməːrk] v.
뽐내듯 웃다

fume [fjuːm] v.
화를 내다

summon [sʌ́mən] v.
부르다, 호출하다

the hand of your daughter for whichever of us may seem good to you and to her. As I have **but** four wives and Brother Drebber here has seven, it appears to me that my claim is the stronger one."

"**Nay**, nay, Brother Stangerson," cried the other; "the question is not how many wives we have, but how many we can keep. My father has now given over his mills to me, and I am the richer man."

"But my prospects are better," said the other, warmly. "When the Lord removes my father, I shall have his tanning yard and his leather factory. Then I am your elder, and am higher in the Church."

"It will be for the maiden to decide," **rejoined** young Drebber, **smirking** at his own reflection in the glass. "We will leave it all to her decision."

During this dialogue John Ferrier had stood **fuming** in the doorway, hardly able to keep his riding-whip from the backs of his two visitors.

"Look here," he said at last, striding up to them, "when my daughter **summons** you, you can come, but until then I don't want to see your faces again."

The two young Mormons stared at him in amazement. In their eyes this competition between them for the maiden's hand was the highest of honours both to her and her father.

"There are two ways out of the room," cried Ferrier; "there is the door, and there is the window. Which do you care to use?"

His brown face looked so savage, and his gaunt hands so threatening, that his visitors sprang to their feet and beat a hurried retreat. The old farmer followed them to the door.

"Let me know when you have settled which it is to be," he said, sardonically.

"You shall **smart** for this!" Stangerson cried, white with rage. "You have **defied** the Prophet and the Council of Four. You shall **rue** it to the end of your days."

"The hand of the Lord shall be heavy upon you," cried young Drebber; "He will arise and **smite** you!"

"Then I'll start the smiting," exclaimed Ferrier, furiously, and would have rushed upstairs for his gun **had not Lucy seized him** by the arm and restrained him. Before

---

smart [smɑːrt] v.
후회하다, 응보를 받다
defy [difái] v.
거부하다, 반대하다, 무시하다
rue [ruː] v.
후회하다
smite [smait] v.
때리다, 벌하다, 혼내주다

had not Lucy seized him:
if Lucy had not seized him

he could escape from her, the clatter of horses' hoofs told him that they were beyond his reach.

"The young **canting rascals**!" he exclaimed, wiping the perspiration from his forehead; "I would sooner see you in your grave, my girl, than the wife of either of them."

"And so should I, father," she answered, with spirit; "but Jefferson will soon be here."

"Yes. It will not be long before he comes. The sooner the better, for we do not know what their next move may be."

It was, indeed, high time that someone capable of giving advice and help should come to the aid of the sturdy old farmer and his adopted daughter. In the whole history of the settlement there had never been such a case of rank disobedience to the authority of the Elders. If minor errors were punished so sternly, what would be the fate of this arch rebel? Ferrier knew that his wealth and position would be of no avail to him. Others as well known and as rich as himself had been spirited away before now, and their

---

canting [kǽntiŋ] adj.
거드름 피우는
rascal [rǽskəl / rɑ́ːs-] n.
악당, 건달

"There are two ways out of the room," cried Ferrier; "there is the door, and there is the window. Which do you care to use?"

unnerve [ʌnnə́ːrv] v.
무기력하게 하다, 불안하게 하다

remonstrance [rimánstr-əns / -mɔ́n-] n.
항의, 충고

straggling [strǽgliŋ] adj.
흐트러진, 산만한, 산재하는, 제각기의

crumple [krʌ́mpl] v.
구기다

goods given over to the Church. He was a brave man, but he trembled at the vague, shadowy terrors which hung over him. Any known danger he could face with a firm lip, but this suspense was **unnerving**. He concealed his fears from his daughter, however, and affected to make light of the whole matter, though she, with the keen eye of love, saw plainly that he was ill at ease.

He expected that he would receive some message or **remonstrance** from Young as to his conduct, and he was not mistaken, though it came in an unlooked-for manner. Upon rising next morning he found, to his surprise, a small square of paper pinned on to the coverlet of his bed just over his chest. On it was printed, in bold **straggling** letters:—

"Twenty-nine days are given you for amendment, and then——"

The dash was more fear-inspiring than any threat could have been. How this warning came into his room puzzled John Ferrier sorely, for his servants slept in an outhouse, and the doors and windows had all been secured. He **crumpled** the

balance [bǽləns] n.
나머지, 잔여
slay [slei] v.
(slay-slew-slain) 살해하다

scrawl [skrɔ:l] v.
휘갈겨 쓰다

paper up and said nothing to his daughter, but the incident struck a chill into his heart. The twenty-nine days were evidently the **balance** of the month which Young had promised. What strength or courage could avail against an enemy armed with such mysterious powers? The hand which fastened that pin might have struck him to the heart, and he could never have known who had **slain** him.

Still more shaken was he next morning. They had sat down to their breakfast, when Lucy with a cry of surprise pointed upwards. In the centre of the ceiling was **scrawled**, with a burned stick apparently, the number 28. To his daughter it was unintelligible, and he did not enlighten her. That night he sat up with his gun and kept watch and ward. He saw and he heard nothing, and yet in the morning a great 27 had been painted upon the outside of his door.

Thus day followed day; and as sure as morning came he found that his unseen enemies had kept their register, and had marked up in some conspicuous position how many days were still left to him out

vigilance [vídʒələns] n. 경계, 불침번
whence [hwens] adv. from where
superstitious [sùːpərstíʃəs] adj. 미신적인
haggard [hǽgərd] adj. 수척한, 초췌한

absentee [æ̀bsəntíː] n. 자리에 없는 사람
dwindle [dwíndl] v. 줄어들다

of the month of grace. Sometimes the fatal numbers appeared upon the walls, sometimes upon the floors, occasionally they were on small placards stuck upon the garden gate or the railings. With all his **vigilance** John Ferrier could not discover **whence** these daily warnings proceeded. A horror which was almost **superstitious** came upon him at the sight of them. He became **haggard** and restless, and his eyes had the troubled look of some hunted creature. He had but one hope in life now, and that was for the arrival of the young hunter from Nevada.

Twenty had changed to fifteen, and fifteen to ten, but there was no news of the **absentee**. One by one the numbers **dwindled** down, and still there came no sign of him. Whenever a horseman clattered down the road, or a driver shouted at his team, the old farmer hurried to the gate, thinking that help had arrived at last. At last, when he saw five give way to four and that again to three, he lost heart, and abandoned all hope of escape. Single-handed, and with his limited knowledge of the mountains which

4 A Flight for Life

surrounded the settlement, he knew that he was powerless. The more frequented roads were strictly watched and guarded, and none could pass along them without an order from the Council. Turn which way he would, there appeared to be no avoiding the blow which hung over him. Yet the old man never **wavered** in his resolution to part with life itself before he consented to what he regarded as his daughter's dishonour.

He was sitting alone one evening pondering deeply over his troubles, and searching vainly for some way out of them. That morning had shown the figure 2 upon the wall of his house, and the next day would be the last of the allotted time. What was to happen then? All manner of vague and terrible fancies filled his imagination. And his daughter—what was to become of her after he was gone? Was there no escape from the invisible network which was drawn all round them? He sank his head upon the table and sobbed at the thought of his own **impotence**.

What was that? In the silence he heard a gentle scratching sound—low, but very

---

waver [wéivəːr] v.
흔들리다, 동요하다

impotence [ímpətəns] n.
무기력, 무능

insidious [insídiəs] adj.
남을 속이는, 교활한
tribunal [traibjúːnl, tri-] n.
재판소

distinct in the quiet of the night. It came from the door of the house. Ferrier crept into the hall and listened intently. There was a pause for a few moments, and then the low, **insidious** sound was repeated. Someone was evidently tapping very gently upon one of the panels of the door. Was it some midnight assassin who had come to carry out the murderous orders of the secret **tribunal**? Or was it some agent who was marking up that the last day of grace had arrived. John Ferrier felt that instant death would be better than the suspense which shook his nerves and chilled his heart. Springing forward, he drew the bolt and threw the door open.

Outside all was calm and quiet. The night was fine, and the stars were twinkling brightly overhead. The little front garden lay before the farmer's eyes bounded by the fence and gate, but neither there nor on the road was any human being to be seen. With a sigh of relief Ferrier looked to right and to left, until, happening to glance straight down at his own feet, he saw to his astonishment a man lying flat upon his face upon the ground, with arms

asprawl [əsprɔ́ːl] adv. adj.
엎드린, 드러누운
stifle [stáif-əl] v.
억누르다
prostrate [prástreit / prɔstréit] adj.
엎드린
writhe [raið] v.
몸을 뒤틀다, 몸부림치다

and legs all **asprawl**.

So unnerved was he at the sight that he leaned up against the wall with his hand to his throat to **stifle** his inclination to call out. His first thought was that the **prostrate** figure was that of some wounded or dying man, but as he watched it he saw it **writhe** along the ground and into the hall with the rapidity and noiselessness of a serpent. Once within the house the

man sprang to his feet, closed the door, and revealed to the astonished farmer the fierce face and resolute expression of Jefferson Hope.

"Good God!" gasped John Ferrier. "How you scared me! Whatever made you come in like that."

"Give me food," the other said, hoarsely. "I have had no time **for bit or sup** for eight-and-forty hours." He flung himself upon the cold meat and bread which were still lying upon the table from his host's supper, and **devoured** it **voraciously**. "Does Lucy **bear up** well?" he asked, when he had satisfied his hunger.

"Yes. She does not know the danger," her father answered.

"That is well. The house is watched on every side. That is why I crawled my way up to it. They may be darned sharp, but they're not quite sharp enough to catch a Washoe hunter."

John Ferrier felt a different man now that he realized that he had a devoted ally. He seized the young man's leathery hand and wrung it cordially. "You're a man to be proud of," he said. "There are

---

for bit or sup: for food or drink
devour [diváuər] v. 게걸스레 먹다
voracious [vouréiʃəs] adj. 식욕이 왕성한
bear up: 견뎌내다, 역경을 이겨내다

not many who would come to share our danger and our troubles."

"You've hit it there, **pard**," the young hunter answered. "I have a respect for you, but if you were alone in this business I'd think twice before I put my head into such **a hornet's nest**. It's Lucy that brings me here, and before harm comes on her I guess there will be one less o' the Hope family in Utah."

"What are we to do?"

"To-morrow is your last day, and unless you act to-night you are lost. I have a mule and two horses waiting in the Eagle Ravine. How much money have you?"

"Two thousand dollars in gold, and five in notes."

"That will do. I have as much more to add to it. We must push for Carson City through the mountains. You had best wake Lucy. It is as well that the servants do not sleep in the house."

While Ferrier was absent, preparing his daughter for the approaching journey, Jefferson Hope packed all the **eatables** that he could find into a small parcel, and filled a stoneware jar with water, for

pard [pɑːrd] n.
동료
hornet's nest: 곤란한 상황

eatable [íːtəbəl] n.
음식

daybreak [déibrèik] n.
동틀녘

he knew by experience that the mountain wells were few and far between. He had hardly completed his arrangements before the farmer returned with his daughter all dressed and ready for a start. The greeting between the lovers was warm, but brief, for minutes were precious, and there was much to be done.

"We must make our start at once," said Jefferson Hope, speaking in a low but resolute voice, like one who realizes the greatness of the peril, but has steeled his heart to meet it. "The front and back entrances are watched, but with caution we may get away through the side window and across the fields. Once on the road we are only two miles from the Ravine where the horses are waiting. By **daybreak** we should be halfway through the mountains."

"What if we are stopped," asked Ferrier.

Hope slapped the revolver butt which protruded from the front of his tunic. "If they are too many for us, we shall take two or three of them with us," he said with a sinister smile.

The lights inside the house had all

outweigh [àutwéi] v.
보다 뛰어나다, 보다 중요하다
lurk [lə:rk] v.
숨어있다

scanty [skǽnti] adj.
부족한
crouch [krautʃ] v.
구부리다, 쪼그리다, 움츠리다

been extinguished, and from the darkened window Ferrier peered over the fields which had been his own, and which he was now about to abandon forever. He had long nerved himself to the sacrifice, however, and the thought of the honour and happiness of his daughter **outweighed** any regret at his ruined fortunes. All looked so peaceful and happy, the rustling trees and the broad silent stretch of grainland, that it was difficult to realize that the spirit of murder **lurked** through it all. Yet the white face and set expression of the young hunter showed that in his approach to the house he had seen enough to satisfy him upon that head.

Ferrier carried the bag of gold and notes, Jefferson Hope had the **scanty** provisions and water, while Lucy had a small bundle containing a few of her more valued possessions. Opening the window very slowly and carefully, they waited until a dark cloud had somewhat obscured the night, and then one by one passed through into the little garden. With bated breath and **crouching** figures they stumbled across it, and gained the shelter of the hedge, which they skirted until they came to the gap which opened into the cornfields. They had just reached this point when the young man seized his two companions and dragged them down into the shadow, where they lay silent and trembling.

It was as well that his prairie training had given Jefferson Hope the ears of a lynx. He and his friends had hardly crouched down before the melancholy **hooting** of a mountain owl was heard within a few yards of them, which was immediately answered by another hoot at a small distance. At the same moment a vague, shadowy figure emerged from the gap for which they had been making, and uttered the **plaintive** signal cry again, on which a second man appeared out of the obscurity.

"To-morrow at midnight," said the first, who appeared to be in authority. "When the Whip-poor-will calls three times."

"It is well," returned the other. "Shall I tell Brother Drebber?"

"Pass it on to him, and from him to

hoot [huːt] v.
(올빼미 등이) 울다
plaintive [pléintiv] adj.
구슬픈

the others. Nine to seven!"

"Seven to five!" repeated the other, and the two figures flitted away in different directions. Their concluding words had evidently been some form of sign and **countersign**. The instant that their footsteps had died away in the distance, Jefferson Hope sprang to his feet, and helping his companions through the gap, led the way across the fields at the top of his speed, supporting and half-carrying the girl when her strength appeared to fail her.

"Hurry on! hurry on!" he gasped from time to time. "We are through the line of **sentinels**. Everything depends on speed. Hurry on!"

Once on the high road, they made rapid progress. Only once did they meet anyone, and then they managed to slip into a field, and so avoid recognition. Before reaching the town the hunter branched away into a rugged and narrow footpath which led to the mountains. Two dark, jagged peaks **loomed** above them through the darkness, and the **defile** which led between them was the Eagle Cañon in which the horses

countersign [káuntərsàin] n. password, 암호

sentinel [séntənəl] n. 보초병, 파수꾼

loom [lu:m] v. 흐릿하게 나타나다
defile [difáil] n. 좁은 골짜기

unerring [ʌnə́:riŋ] adj.
실수하지 않는
picket [píkit] v.
말뚝에 매다
precipitous [prisípətəs] adj. 절벽의, 깎아지른 듯한

crag [kræg] n.
우뚝 솟은 험한 바위
tower [táuə:r] v.
높이 솟다
menacing [ménəsiŋ] adj.
위협적인
petrify [pétrəfài] v.
돌이 되다, 딱딱하게 되다
chaos [kéiɑs / -ɔs] n.
무질서, 혼란
debris [dəbrí:, déibri: / déb-] n.
파편, 잔해
indian file:
일렬종대
fugitive [fjú:dʒətiv] n.
도망자

were awaiting them. With **unerring** instinct Jefferson Hope picked his way among the great boulders and along the bed of a dried-up watercourse, until he came to the retired corner, screened with rocks, where the faithful animals had been **picketed**. The girl was placed upon the mule, and old Ferrier upon one of the horses, with his money-bag, while Jefferson Hope led the other along the **precipitous** and dangerous path.

It was a bewildering route for anyone who was not accustomed to face Nature in her wildest moods. On the one side a great **crag towered** up a thousand feet or more, black, stern, and **menacing**, with long basaltic columns upon its rugged surface like the ribs of some **petrified** monster. On the other hand a wild **chaos** of boulders and **debris** made all advance impossible. Between the two ran the irregular track, so narrow in places that they had to travel in **Indian file**, and so rough that only practised riders could have traversed it at all. Yet, in spite of all dangers and difficulties, the hearts of the **fugitives** were light within them,

4 A Flight for Life 217

despotism [déspətìzəm] n.
전제정치, 독재정치

jurisdiction
[dʒùərisdíkʃən] n.
권력, 사법권

for every step increased the distance between them and the terrible **despotism** from which they were flying.

They soon had a proof, however, that they were still within the **jurisdiction** of the Saints. They had reached the very wildest and most desolate portion of the pass when the girl gave a startled cry, and pointed upwards. On a rock which overlooked the track, showing out dark and plain against the sky, there stood a solitary sentinel. He saw them as soon as they perceived him, and his military challenge of "Who goes there?" rang through the silent ravine.

"Travellers for Nevada," said Jefferson Hope, with his hand upon the rifle which hung by his saddle.

They could see the lonely watcher fingering his gun, and peering down at them as if dissatisfied at their reply.

"By whose permission?" he asked.

"The Holy Four," answered Ferrier. His Mormon experiences had taught him that that was the highest authority to which he could refer.

"Nine to seven," cried the sentinel.

"Seven to five," returned Jefferson Hope promptly, remembering the countersign which he had heard in the garden.

"Pass, and the Lord go with you," said the voice from above. Beyond his post the path broadened out, and the horses were able to break into a trot. Looking back, they could see the solitary watcher leaning upon his gun, and knew that they had passed the **outlying** post of the

outlying [áutlàiiŋ] adj.
외부의, 외딴

"Nine to seven," cried the sentinel.
"Seven to five," returned Jefferson Hope promptly, remembering the countersign which he had heard in the garden.

chosen people, and that freedom lay before them.

5 The Avenging Angels

intricate [íntrəkit] adj.
뒤엉킨, 복잡한
intimate [íntəmit] adj.
친밀한, 개인적인
hem [hem] v.
둘러싸다

All night their course lay through **intricate** defiles and over irregular and rockstrewn paths. More than once they lost their way, but Hope's **intimate** knowledge of the mountains enabled them to regain the track once more. When morning broke, a scene of marvellous though savage beauty lay before them. In every direction the great snow-capped peaks **hemmed** them in, peeping over each other's shoulders to the far horizon. So steep were the rocky banks on either side of them that the larch and the pine seemed to be suspended over their

hurtle [hə́ːrtl] v. 돌진하다	
gorge [gɔːrʤ] n. 산골짜기	

heads, and to need only a gust of wind to come **hurtling** down upon them. Nor was the fear entirely an illusion, for the barren valley was thickly strewn with trees and boulders which had fallen in a similar manner. Even as they passed, a great rock came thundering down with a hoarse rattle which woke the echoes in the silent **gorges**, and startled the weary horses into a gallop.

ruddy [rʌ́di] adj. 불그레한
partake [pɑːrtéik] v. 함께 하다, 나누다
fain [fein] adj. adv. 기꺼이, 쾌히
inexorable [inéksərəbəl] adj. 가차없는, 움직이지 않는

As the sun rose slowly above the eastern horizon, the caps of the great mountains lit up one after the other, like lamps at a festival, until they were all **ruddy** and glowing. The magnificent spectacle cheered the hearts of the three fugitives and gave them fresh energy. At a wild torrent which swept out of a ravine they called a halt and watered their horses, while they **partook** of a hasty breakfast. Lucy and her father would **fain** have rested longer, but Jefferson Hope was **inexorable**. "They will be upon our track by this time," he said. "Everything depends upon our speed. Once safe in Carson, we may rest for the remainder of our lives."

beetling [bíːtliŋ] adj.
돌출한, 튀어나온
enmity [énməti] n.
적의, 증오
incur [inkə́ːr] v.
(좋지 않은 결과에) 빠지다,
(손해 등을) 초래하다

scanty [skǽnti] adj.
부족한, 불충분한
provisions [prəvíʒən] n.
식량, 음식
nook [nuk] n.
구석

During the whole of that day they struggled on through the defiles, and by evening they calculated that they were more than thirty miles from their enemies. At night-time they chose the base of a **beetling** crag, where the rocks offered some protection from the chill wind, and there, huddled together for warmth, they enjoyed a few hours' sleep. Before daybreak, however, they were up and on their way once more. They had seen no signs of any pursuers, and Jefferson Hope began to think that they were fairly out of the reach of the terrible organization whose **enmity** they had **incurred**. He little knew how far that iron grasp could reach, or how soon it was to close upon them and crush them.

About the middle of the second day of their flight their **scanty** store of **provisions** began to run out. This gave the hunter little uneasiness, however, for there was game to be had among the mountains, and he had frequently before had to depend upon his rifle for the needs of life. Choosing a sheltered **nook**, he piled together a few dried branches and

tether [téðə:r] v.
매어 놓다
crouch [krautʃ] v.
구부리다, 쭈그리다, 움츠리다

ravine [rəvíːn] n.
계곡, 협곡

made a blazing fire, at which his companions might warm themselves, for they were now nearly five thousand feet above the sea level, and the air was bitter and keen. Having **tethered** the horses, and bade Lucy adieu, he threw his gun over his shoulder, and set out in search of whatever chance might throw in his way. Looking back, he saw the old man and the young girl **crouching** over the blazing fire, while the three animals stood motionless in the background. Then the intervening rocks hid them from his view.

He walked for a couple of miles through one **ravine** after another without success, though, from the marks upon the bark of the trees, and other indications, he judged that there were numerous bears in the vicinity. At last, after two or three hours' fruitless search, he was thinking of turning back in despair, when casting his eyes upwards he saw a sight which sent a thrill of pleasure through his heart. On the edge of a jutting pinnacle, three or four hundred feet above him, there stood a creature somewhat resembling a sheep in appearance, but armed with

precipice [présəpis] n.
벼랑, 절벽

unwieldy [ʌnwíːldi] adj.
다루기 어려운, 거추장스
러운

a pair of gigantic horns. The big-horn—for so it is called—was acting, probably, as a guardian over a flock which were invisible to the hunter; but fortunately it was heading in the opposite direction, and had not perceived him. Lying on his face, he rested his rifle upon a rock, and took a long and steady aim before drawing the trigger. The animal sprang into the air, tottered for a moment upon the edge of the **precipice**, and then came crashing down into the valley beneath.

The creature was too **unwieldy** to lift, so the hunter contented himself with cutting away one haunch and part of the flank. With this trophy over his shoulder, he hastened to retrace his steps, for the evening was already drawing in. He had hardly started, however, before he realized the difficulty which faced him. In his eagerness he had wandered far past the ravines which were known to him, and it was no easy matter to pick out the path which he had taken. The valley in which he found himself divided and sub-divided into many gorges, which were so like each other that it was impossible to distinguish one from the other. He followed one for a mile or more until he came to a mountain torrent which he was sure that he had never seen before. Convinced that he had taken the wrong turn, he tried another, but with the same result. Night was coming on rapidly, and it was almost dark before he at last found himself in a defile which was familiar to him. Even then it was no easy matter to keep to the right track, for the moon had not yet risen, and the high cliffs on either side made the obscurity more profound. Weighed down with his burden, and weary from his exertions, he stumbled along, keeping up his heart by the reflection that every step brought him nearer to Lucy, and that he carried with him enough to ensure them food for the remainder of their journey.

He had now come to the mouth of the very defile in which he had left them. Even in the darkness he could recognize the outline of the cliffs which bounded it. They must, he reflected, be awaiting him anxiously, for he had been absent nearly five hours. In the gladness of his heart he

glen [glen] n.
골짜기
reecho [ri(:)ékou] v.
음이 반향하다, 울려퍼지다
save [seiv] prep.
~을 제외하고

tend [tend] v.
돌보다
disaster [dizǽstər, -zάːs-]
n. 재해, 참사, 큰 불운

put his hands to his mouth and made the **glen reecho** to a loud halloo as a signal that he was coming. He paused and listened for an answer. None came **save** his own cry, which clattered up the dreary, silent ravines, and was borne back to his ears in countless repetitions. Again he shouted, even louder than before, and again no whisper came back from the friends whom he had left such a short time ago. A vague, nameless dread came over him, and he hurried onwards frantically, dropping the precious food in his agitation.

When he turned the corner, he came full in sight of the spot where the fire had been lit. There was still a glowing pile of wood ashes there, but it had evidently not been **tended** since his departure. The same dead silence still reigned all round. With his fears all changed to convictions, he hurried on. There was no living creature near the remains of the fire: animals, man, maiden, all were gone. It was only too clear that some sudden and terrible **disaster** had occurred during his absence—a disaster which had embraced them all,

bewilder [biwíldər] v.
당황하다
overtake [òuvərtéik] v.
따라잡다
fugitive [fjú:dʒətiv] n.
도주자, 도피자

and yet had left no traces behind it.

Bewildered and stunned by this blow, Jefferson Hope felt his head spin round, and had to lean upon his rifle to save himself from falling. He was essentially a man of action, however, and speedily recovered from his temporary impotence. Seizing a half-consumed piece of wood from the smouldering fire, he blew it into a flame, and proceeded with its help to examine the little camp. The ground was all stamped down by the feet of horses, showing that a large party of mounted men had **overtaken** the **fugitives**, and the direction of their tracks proved that they had afterwards turned back to Salt Lake City. Had they carried back both of his companions with them? Jefferson Hope had almost persuaded himself that they must have done so, when his eye fell upon an object which made every nerve of his body tingle within him. A little way on one side of the camp was a low-lying heap of reddish soil, which had assuredly not been there before. There was no mistaking it for anything but a newly dug grave. As the young hunter approached it, he perceived that a stick had been planted on it, with a sheet of paper stuck in the cleft fork of it. The inscription upon the paper was brief, but to the point:

JOHN FERRIER,
FORMERLY OF SALT LAKE CITY,
Died August 4th, 1860.

The **sturdy** old man, whom he had left so short a time before, was gone, then, and this was all his **epitaph**. Jefferson Hope looked wildly round to see if there was a second grave, but there was no sign of one. Lucy had been carried back by their terrible pursuers to fulfil her original destiny, by becoming one of the harem of an Elder's son. As the young fellow realized the certainty of her fate, and his own powerlessness to prevent it, he wished that he, too, was lying with the old farmer in his last silent resting-place.

Again, however, his active spirit shook off the **lethargy** which springs from despair. If there was nothing else left to him, he could at least devote his life to

indomitable
[indámətəbəl / -dóm-] adj.
꺾이지 않는, 굴복하지 않는
perseverance
[pə̀ːrsəvíːrəns] n.
인내, 끈기
vindictiveness [vindíktivnis] n.
복수
assuage [əswéidʒ] v.
누그러뜨리다, 완화시키다
retribution [rètrəbjúːʃ-ən] n. 앙갚음, 보복

revenge. With **indomitable** patience and **perseverance**, Jefferson Hope possessed also a power of sustained **vindictiveness**, which he may have learned from the Indians amongst whom he had lived. As he stood by the desolate fire, he felt that the only one thing which could **assuage** his grief would be thorough and complete **retribution**, brought by his own hand upon his enemies. His strong will and

The sturdy old man, whom he had left so short a time before, was gone, then, and this was all his epitaph.

untiring energy should, he determined, be devoted to that one end. With a grim, white face, he retraced his steps to where he had dropped the food, and having stirred up the smouldering fire, he cooked enough to last him for a few days. This he made up into a bundle, and, tired as he was, he set himself to walk back through the mountains upon the track of the Avenging Angels.

For five days he **toiled footsore** and weary through the defiles which he had already traversed on horseback. At night he flung himself down among the rocks, and snatched a few hours of sleep; but before daybreak he was always well on his way. On the sixth day, he reached the Eagle Cañon, from which they had commenced their ill-fated flight. **Thence** he could look down upon the home of the Saints. Worn and exhausted, he leaned upon his rifle and shook his gaunt hand fiercely at the silent widespread city beneath him. As he looked at it, he observed that there were flags in some of the principal streets, and other signs of festivity. He was still speculating **as**

---

toil [tɔil] v.
힘써 일하다, 힘들게 걷다
footsore [fútsɔ̀:r] adj.
(많이 걸어) 발이 아픈
thence [ðens] adv.
거기서부터, 그 때부터
as to ~:
~에 관하여

5 The Avenging Angels

to what this might mean when he heard the clatter of horse's hoofs, and saw a mounted man riding towards him. As he approached, he recognized him as a Mormon named Cowper, to whom he had rendered services at different times. He therefore **accosted** him when he got up to him, with the object of finding out what Lucy Ferrier's fate had been.

"I am Jefferson Hope," he said. "You remember me."

The Mormon looked at him with undisguised astonishment—indeed, it was difficult to recognize in this **tattered**, **unkempt** wanderer, with ghastly white face and fierce, wild eyes, the **spruce** young hunter of former days. Having, however, at last, satisfied himself as to his identity, the man's surprise changed to **consternation**.

"You are mad to come here," he cried. "It is as much as my own life is worth to be seen talking with you. There is a **warrant** against you from the Holy Four for assisting the Ferriers away."

"I don't fear them, or their warrant," Hope said, earnestly. "You must know

---

accost [əkɔ́(:)st, əkást] v.
접근하다, 말 걸다

tattered [tǽtəːrd] adj.
남루한, 너덜너덜한
unkempt [ʌnkémpt] adj.
흐트러진, 헝클어진, 단정치 못한
spruce [spruːs] adj.
깔끔한, 말쑥한
consternation [kànstərnéiʃən / kɔ̀n-] n.
경악, 대경실색

warrant [wɔ́(:)rənt, wár-]
n. 명령, 영장

conjure [kándʒər, kʌ́n-] v.
간청하다, 탄원하다

something of this matter, Cowper. I **conjure** you by everything you hold dear to answer a few questions. We have always been friends. For God's sake, don't refuse to answer me."

"What is it?" the Mormon asked, uneasily. "Be quick. The very rocks have ears and the trees eyes."

"What has become of Lucy Ferrier?"

"She was married yesterday to young Drebber. Hold up, man, hold up; you have no life left in you."

"Don't mind me," said Hope faintly. He was white to the very lips, and had sunk down on the stone against which he had been leaning. "Married, you say?"

"Married yesterday—that's what those flags are for on the Endowment House. There was some words between young Drebber and young Stangerson as to which was to have her. They'd both been in the party that followed them, and Stangerson had shot her father, which seemed to give him the best claim; but when they argued it out in council, Drebber's party was the stronger, so the Prophet gave her over to him. No one won't have her very long though, for I saw death in her face yesterday. She is more like a ghost than a woman. Are you off, then?"

"Yes, I am off," said Jefferson Hope, who had risen from his seat. His face might have been **chiselled** out of marble, so hard and set was its expression, while its eyes glowed with a **baleful** light.

"Where are you going?"

"Never mind," he answered; and, slinging his weapon over his shoulder, strode off down the gorge and so away into the heart of the mountains to the haunts of the wild beasts. Amongst them all there was none so fierce and so dangerous as himself.

The prediction of the Mormon was only too well fulfilled. Whether it was the terrible death of her father or the effects of the hateful marriage into which she had been forced, poor Lucy never held up her head again, but pined away and died within a month. Her **sottish** husband, who had married her principally **for the sake of** John Ferrier's property, did not affect any great grief

bereavement [birí:vmənt] n. 여읨, 사별
bier [biər] n. 관가(棺架), 관대
snarl [snɑ:rl] n. 으르렁거림, 딱딱거림
had it not been for: if it had not been for

at his **bereavement**; but his other wives mourned over her, and sat up with her the night before the burial, as is the Mormon custom. They were grouped round the **bier** in the early hours of the morning, when, to their inexpressible fear and astonishment, the door was flung open, and a savage-looking, weather-beaten man in tattered garments strode into the room. Without a glance or a word to the cowering women, he walked up to the white silent figure which had once contained the pure soul of Lucy Ferrier. Stooping over her, he pressed his lips reverently to her cold forehead, and then, snatching up her hand, he took the wedding ring from her finger. "She shall not be buried in that," he cried with a fierce **snarl**, and before an alarm could be raised sprang down the stairs and was gone. So strange and so brief was the episode that the watchers might have found it hard to believe it themselves or persuade other people of it, **had it not been for** the undeniable fact that the circlet of gold which marked her as having been a bride had disappeared.

prowl [praul] v.
헤매다, 서성거리다
boulder [bóuldər] n.
둥근 돌, 바위
expedition [èkspədíʃən] n.
(집단, 단체의) 모험, 원정
nightfall [náitfɔ̀:l] n.
해질녘
vindictiveness [vindík-tivnis] n.
복수

"She shall not be buried in that," he cried with a fierce snarl...

For some months Jefferson Hope lingered among the mountains, leading a strange, wild life, and nursing in his heart the fierce desire for vengeance which possessed him. Tales were told in the City of the weird figure which was seen **prowling** about the suburbs, and which haunted the lonely mountain gorges. Once a bullet whistled through Stangerson's window and flattened itself upon the wall within a foot of him. On another occasion, as Drebber passed under a cliff a great **boulder** crashed down on him, and he only escaped a terrible death by throwing himself upon his face. The two young Mormons were not long in discovering the reason of these attempts upon their lives, and led repeated **expeditions** into the mountains in the hope of capturing or killing their enemy, but always without success. Then they adopted the precaution of never going out alone or after **nightfall**, and of having their houses guarded. After a time they were able to relax these measures, for nothing was either heard or seen of their opponent, and they hoped that time had cooled his **vindictiveness**.

augment [ɔ:gmént] v.
늘리다, 증대하다
predominant [pridámənənt / -dɔ́m-] adj.
우세한, 우월한, 지배적인
constitution [kànstətjúːʃən / kɔ̀n-] n.
체격, 체질
incessant [insésənt] adj.
끊임없는, 계속되는
want [wɔ(:)nt, wɑnt] n.
결핍, 부족
wholesome [hóulsəm] adj.
건전한, 유익한
overtake [òuvərtéik] v.
불시에 닥쳐오다, 갑자기 일어나다
privation [praivéiʃən] n.
결핍, 박탈

Far from doing so, it had, if anything, **augmented** it. The hunter's mind was of a hard, unyielding nature, and the **predominant** idea of revenge had taken such complete possession of it that there was no room for any other emotion. He was, however, above all things, practical. He soon realized that even his iron **constitution** could not stand the **incessant** strain which he was putting upon it. Exposure and **want** of **wholesome** food were wearing him out. If he died like a dog among the mountains, what was to become of his revenge then? And yet such a death was sure to **overtake** him if he persisted. He felt that that was to play his enemy's game, so he reluctantly returned to the old Nevada mines, there to recruit his health and to amass money enough to allow him to pursue his object without **privation**.

His intention had been to be absent a year at the most, but a combination of unforeseen circumstances prevented his leaving the mines for nearly five. At the end of that time, however, his memory of his wrongs and his craving for revenge

assumed [əsjú:md] adj.
가짜의, 가공의
tiding [taidiŋ] n.
소식, 정보, 뉴스
schism [síz-əm, skíz-] n.
분열
secession [siséʃ-ən] n.
탈퇴, 탈당
malcontent [mǽlkəntént] n. 불만을 품은 사람, 반항자
whither [hwíðə:r] adv. conj.
어디로

falter [fɔ́:ltər] v.
비틀거리다, 주저하다

were quite as keen as on that memorable night when he had stood by John Ferrier's grave. Disguised, and under an **assumed** name, he returned to Salt Lake City, careless what became of his own life, as long as he obtained what he knew to be justice. There he found evil **tidings** awaiting him. There had been a **schism** among the Chosen People a few months before, some of the younger members of the Church having rebelled against the authority of the Elders, and the result had been the **secession** of a certain number of the **malcontents**, who had left Utah and become Gentiles. Among these had been Drebber and Stangerson; and no one knew **whither** they had gone. Rumour reported that Drebber had managed to convert a large part of his property into money, and that he had departed a wealthy man, while his companion, Stangerson, was comparatively poor. There was no clue at all, however, as to their whereabouts.

Many a man, however vindictive, would have abandoned all thought of revenge in the face of such a difficulty, but Jefferson Hope never **faltered** for a moment. With

competence
[kámpətəns / kɔ́m-] n.
충분한 재산, 소득
eke [i:k] v.
보충하다, 꾸려나가다
perseverance
[pə̀:rsəvíːrəns]: n.
인내, 끈기, 버팀
vagrant [véigrənt] n.
부랑자, 정처없는 사람
justice of the peace:
치안 판사
custody [kʌ́stədi] n.
감금, 구류
surety [ʃúərti, ʃúərəti] n.
보증, 담보
detain [ditéin] v.
붙들다, 구류하다

the small **competence** he possessed, **eked** out by such employment as he could pick up, he travelled from town to town through the United States in quest of his enemies. Year passed into year, his black hair turned grizzled, but still he wandered on, a human bloodhound, with his mind wholly set upon the one object to which he had devoted his life. At last his **perseverance** was rewarded. It was but a glance of a face in a window, but that one glance told him that Cleveland in Ohio possessed the men whom he was in pursuit of. He returned to his miserable lodgings with his plan of vengeance all arranged. It chanced, however, that Drebber, looking from his window, had recognized the **vagrant** in the street, and had read murder in his eyes. He hurried before **a justice of the peace** accompanied by Stangerson, who had become his private secretary, and represented to him that they were in danger of their lives from the jealousy and hatred of an old rival. That evening Jefferson Hope was taken into **custody**, and not being able to find **sureties**, was **detained** for some weeks. When at last he was liberated, it was only to find that Drebber's house was deserted, and that he and his secretary had departed for Europe.

Again the avenger had been **foiled**, and again his concentrated hatred urged him to continue the pursuit. Funds were wanting, however, and for some time he had to return to work, saving every dollar for his approaching journey. At last, having collected enough to keep life in him, he departed for Europe, and tracked his enemies from city to city, working his way in any **menial** capacity, but never overtaking the fugitives. When he reached St. Petersburg, they had departed for Paris; and when he followed them there, he learned that they had just set off for Copenhagen. At the Danish capital he was again a few days late, for they had journeyed on to London, where he at last succeeded in running them to earth. As to what occurred there, we cannot do better than quote the old hunter's own account, as duly recorded in Dr. Watson's Journal, to which we are already under such obligations.

foil [fɔil] v.
좌절시키다
menial [míːniəl, -njəl] adj.
하인의, 비천한

6 A Continuation of the Reminiscences of John Watson, M.D.

reminiscence [rèmənís-əns] n.
회고, 회상
M.D.:
(Latin) Medicinae Doctor (Doctor of Medicine), 의학박사

ferocity [fərásəti / -rɔ́s-] n.
잔인함, 포악성
disposition [dìspəzíʃən] n.
기질, 성미, 성격, 취향
affable [ǽfəbəl] adj.
붙임성 있는
scuffle [skʌ́f-əl] v.
드잡이, 난투

Our prisoner's furious resistance did not apparently indicate any **ferocity** in his **disposition** towards ourselves, for on finding himself powerless, he smiled in an **affable** manner, and expressed his hopes that he had not hurt any of us in the **scuffle**. "I guess you're going to take me to the police-station," he remarked to Sherlock Holmes. "My cab's at the door. If you'll loose my legs I'll walk down to it. I'm not so light to lift as I used to be."

Gregson and Lestrade exchanged glances, as if they thought this proposition rather a bold one; but Holmes at once took the prisoner at his word, and loosened the towel which we had bound round his ankles. He rose and stretched his legs, as though to assure himself that they were free once more. I remember that I thought to myself, as I eyed him, that I had seldom seen a more powerfully built man; and his dark, sunburned face bore an expression of determination and energy which was as formidable as his personal strength.

"If there's a vacant place for a chief of the police, I **reckon** you are the man for it," he said, gazing with undisguised admiration at my fellow-lodger. "The way you kept on my trail was a **caution**."

"You had better come with me," said Holmes to the two detectives.

"I can drive you," said Lestrade.

"Good! and Gregson can come inside with me. You too, Doctor, you have taken an interest in the case, and may as well stick to us."

reckon [rék-ən] v.
생각하다, 간주하다
caution [kɔ́:ʃən] n.
놀라운 일 또는 사람

assent [əsént] v.
동의하다, 찬성하다
usher [ʌ́ʃər] v.
안내하다
magistrate [mǽdʒəstrèit, -trit] n.
법관, 판사

I **assented** gladly, and we all descended together. Our prisoner made no attempt at escape, but stepped calmly into the cab which had been his, and we followed him. Lestrade mounted the box, whipped up the horse, and brought us in a very short time to our destination. We were **ushered** into a small chamber, where a police inspector noted down our prisoner's name and the names of the men with whose murder he had been charged. The official was a white-faced, unemotional man, who went through his duties in a dull, mechanical way. "The prisoner will be put before the **magistrates** in the course of the week," he said; "in the meantime, Mr. Jefferson Hope, have you anything that you wish to say? I must warn you that your words will be taken down, and may be used against you."

"I've got a good deal to say," our prisoner said slowly. "I want to tell you gentlemen all about it."

"Hadn't you better reserve that for your trial?" asked the inspector.

"I may never be tried," he answered. "You needn't look startled. It isn't suicide

I am thinking of. Are you a Doctor?" He turned his fierce dark eyes upon me as he asked this last question.

"Yes; I am," I answered.

"Then put your hand here," he said, with a smile, motioning with his **manacled** wrists towards his chest.

I did so; and became at once conscious of an extraordinary **throbbing** and **commotion** which was going on inside. The

manacle [mǽnəkl] v.
수갑을 채우다, 족쇄를 채우다
throb [θrɑb / θrɔb] v.
(심장 등이) 고동치다, 두근거리다
commotion [kəmóuʃən] n.
격렬한 움직임, 동요, 흥분

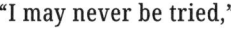

"I may never be tried,"

frail [freil] adj. 허약한	walls of his chest seemed to thrill and quiver as a **frail** building would do inside when some powerful engine was at work. In the silence of the room I could hear a dull humming and buzzing noise which proceeded from the same source.
aortic aneurism: 대동맥류, 대동맥의 벽이 약화되어 대동맥이 부분적으로 커지는 증상 placid [plǽsid] adj. 조용한, 평온한 account [əkáunt] n. 이야기, 기술, 서술, 보고	"Why," I cried, "you have an **aortic aneurism**!" "That's what they call it," he said, **placidly**. "I went to a Doctor last week about it, and he told me that it is bound to burst before many days passed. It has been getting worse for years. I got it from over-exposure and under-feeding among the Salt Lake Mountains. I've done my work now, and I don't care how soon I go, but I should like to leave some **account** of the business behind me. I don't want to be remembered as a common cut-throat."

The inspector and the two detectives had a hurried discussion as to the advisability of allowing him to tell his story.

"Do you consider, Doctor, that there is immediate danger?" the former asked.

"Most certainly there is," I answered.

"In that case it is clearly our duty, in the interests of justice, to take his

leave [liːv] n.
허락, 허가
tussle [tʌs-əl] n.
난투, 드잡이
brink [briŋk] n.
가장자리, 언저리

vouch [vautʃ] v.
보장하다
subjoin [səbdʒɔ́in] v.
더하다, 추가하다

forfeit [fɔ́ːrfit] v.
잃다, 몰수당하다

statement," said the inspector. "You are at liberty, sir, to give your account, which I again warn you will be taken down."

"I'll sit down, with your **leave**," the prisoner said, suiting the action to the word. "This aneurism of mine makes me easily tired, and the **tussle** we had half an hour ago has not mended matters. I'm on the **brink** of the grave, and I am not likely to lie to you. Every word I say is the absolute truth, and how you use it is a matter of no consequence to me."

With these words, Jefferson Hope leaned back in his chair and began the following remarkable statement. He spoke in a calm and methodical manner, as though the events which he narrated were commonplace enough. I can **vouch** for the accuracy of the **subjoined** account, for I have had access to Lestrade's notebook, in which the prisoner's words were taken down exactly as they were uttered.

"It don't much matter to you why I hated these men," he said; "it's enough that they were guilty of the death of two human beings—a father and a daughter—and that they had, therefore, **forfeited** their own lives. After the lapse of time that has passed since their crime, it was impossible for me to secure a conviction against them in any court. I knew of their guilt though, and I determined that I should be judge, jury, and executioner all rolled into one. You'd have done the same, if you have any manhood in you, if you had been in my place.

"That girl that I spoke of was to have married me twenty years ago. She was forced into marrying that same Drebber, and broke her heart over it. I took the marriage ring from her dead finger, and I vowed that his dying eyes should rest upon that very ring, and that his last thoughts should be of the crime for which he was punished. I have carried it about with me, and have followed him and his **accomplice** over two continents until I caught them. They thought to tire me out, but they could not do it. If I die to-morrow, as is likely enough, I die knowing that my work in this world is done, and well done. They have perished, and by my hand. There is nothing left for me to hope for, or to desire.

---

accomplice [əkámplis / əkʌ́m-] n.
공범

reckon [rék-ən] v.
생각하다, 간주하다
maze [meiz] n.
미로, 미궁
contrive [kəntráiv] v.
고안하다, 설계하다

"They were rich and I was poor, so that it was no easy matter for me to follow them. When I got to London my pocket was about empty, and I found that I must turn my hand to something for my living. Driving and riding are as natural to me as walking, so I applied at a cab-owner's office, and soon got employment. I was to bring a certain sum a week to the owner, and whatever was over that I might keep for myself. There was seldom much over, but I managed to scrape along somehow. The hardest job was to learn my way about, for I **reckon** that of all the **mazes** that ever were **contrived**, this city is the most confusing. I had a map beside me, though, and when once I had spotted the principal hotels and stations, I got on pretty well.

"It was some time before I found out where my two gentlemen were living; but I inquired and inquired until at last I dropped across them. They were at a boarding-house at Camberwell, over on the other side of the river. When once I found them out, I knew that I had them at my mercy. I had grown my beard, and there was no chance of their recognizing me. I would dog them and follow them until I saw my opportunity. I was determined that they should not escape me again.

"They were very near doing it for all that. Go where they would about London, I was always **at their heels**. Sometimes I followed them on my cab, and sometimes on foot, but the former was the best, for then they could not get away from me.

"It was only early in the morning or late at night that I could earn anything, so that I began to get behind hand with my employer. I did not mind that, however, as long as I could lay my hand upon the men I wanted.

"They were very cunning, though. They must have thought that there was some chance of their being followed, for they would never go out alone, and never after nightfall. During two weeks I drove behind them every day, and never once saw them separate. Drebber himself was drunk half the time, but Stangerson was not to **be caught napping**. I watched

---

at one's heels:
누구를 뒤쫓아,

catch someone napping:
기습하다, 허를 찌르다

ghost [goust] n.
극히 적은 가능성, 조금, 극소

ill at ease:
불편한, 초조한, 불안한
quarters [kwɔ́ːrtər] n.
숙소, 주거

them late and early, but never saw the **ghost** of a chance; but I was not discouraged, for something told me that the hour had almost come. My only fear was that this thing in my chest might burst a little too soon and leave my work undone.

"At last, one evening I was driving up and down Torquay Terrace, as the street was called in which they boarded, when I saw a cab drive up to their door. Presently some luggage was brought out and after a time Drebber and Stangerson followed it, and drove off. I whipped up my horse and kept within sight of them, feeling very **ill at ease**, for I feared that they were going to shift their **quarters**. At Euston Station they got out, and I left a boy to hold my horse, and followed them on to the platform. I heard them ask for the Liverpool train, and the guard answer that one had just gone, and there would not be another for some hours. Stangerson seemed to be put out at that, but Drebber was rather pleased than otherwise. I got so close to them in the bustle that I could hear every word that passed between them. Drebber said that

remonstrate [rimánstreit, rémənstrèit / rimɔ́nstreit] v. 항의하다, 불만을 말하다

undue [ʌndjúː / -djúː] adj. 적절하지 않은, 마땅치 않은, 지나친, 과도한
precipitation [prisìpətéiʃən] n. 조급함, 경솔함

he had a little business of his own to do, and that if the other would wait for him he would soon rejoin him. His companion **remonstrated** with him, and reminded him that they had resolved to stick together. Drebber answered that the matter was a delicate one, and that he must go alone. I could not catch what Stangerson said to that, but the other burst out swearing, and reminded him that he was nothing more than his paid servant, and that he must not presume to dictate to him. On that the Secretary gave it up as a bad job, and simply bargained with him that if he missed the last train he should rejoin him at Halliday's Private Hotel; to which Drebber answered that he would be back on the platform before eleven, and made his way out of the station.

"The moment for which I had waited so long had at last come. I had my enemies within my power. Together they could protect each other, but singly they were at my mercy. I did not act, however, with **undue precipitation**. My plans were already formed. There is no satisfaction in vengeance unless the offender has time to realize who it is that strikes him, and why retribution has come upon him. I had my plans arranged by which I should have the opportunity of making the man who had wronged me understand that his old sin had found him out. It chanced that some days before a gentleman who had been engaged in looking over some houses in the Brixton Road had dropped the key of one of them in my carriage. It was claimed that same evening, and returned; but in the interval I had taken a moulding of it, and had a duplicate constructed. By means of this I had access to at least one spot in this great city where I could rely upon being free from interruption. How to get Drebber to that house was the difficult problem which I had now to solve.

"He walked down the road and went into one or two liquor shops, staying for nearly half an hour in the last of them. When he came out, he staggered in his walk, and was evidently pretty well on. There was a hansom just in front of me, and he hailed it. I followed it so close that the nose of my horse was within a yard of his driver the whole way. We rattled across Waterloo Bridge and through miles of streets, until, to my astonishment, we found ourselves back in the terrace in which he had boarded. I could not imagine what his intention was in returning there; but I went on and pulled up my cab a hundred yards or so from the house. He entered it, and his hansom drove away. Give me a glass of water, if you please. My mouth gets dry with the talking."

I handed him the glass, and he drank it down.

"That's better," he said. "Well, I waited for a quarter of an hour, or more, when suddenly there came a noise like people struggling inside the house. Next moment the door was flung open and two men appeared, one of whom was Drebber, and the other was **a young chap** whom I had never seen before. This fellow had Drebber by the collar, and when they came to the head of the steps he gave him a **shove** and a kick which sent him half across the road. 'You hound,' he

---

a young chap:
Arthur Charpentier

shove [ʃʌv] n.
떠밀기

thrash [θræʃ] v.
때리다
cudgel [kʌdʒəl] n.
곤봉
cur [kəːr] n.
잡종개, 망나니

cried, shaking his stick at him; 'I'll teach you to insult an honest girl!' He was so hot that I think he would have **thrashed** Drebber with his **cudgel**, only that the **cur** staggered away down the road as fast as his legs would carry him. He ran as far as the corner, and then, seeing my cab, he hailed me and jumped in. 'Drive me to Halliday's Private Hotel,' said he.

"When I had him fairly inside my cab, my heart jumped so with joy that I feared lest at this last moment my aneurism might go wrong. I drove along slowly, weighing in my own mind what it was best to do. I might take him right out into the country, and there in some deserted lane have my last interview with him. I had almost decided upon this, when he solved the problem for me. The craze for drink had seized him again, and he ordered me to pull up outside a gin palace. He went in, leaving word that I should wait for him. There he remained until closing time, and when he came out he was so far gone that I knew the game was in my own hands.

billet [bílit] n.
일, 직업
extract [ikstrǽkt] v.
뽑아내다, 추출하다
draw [drɔ:] n.
제비(뽑기)

"Don't imagine that I intended to kill him in cold blood. It would only have been rigid justice if I had done so, but I could not bring myself to do it. I had long determined that he should have a show for his life if he chose to take advantage of it. Among the many **billets** which I have filled in America during my wandering life, I was once janitor and sweeper out of the laboratory at York College. One day the professor was lecturing on poisons, and he showed his students some alkaloid, as he called it, which he had **extracted** from some South American arrow poison, and which was so powerful that the least grain meant instant death. I spotted the bottle in which this preparation was kept, and when they were all gone, I helped myself to a little of it. I was a fairly good dispenser, so I worked this alkaloid into small, soluble pills, and each pill I put in a box with a similar pill made without the poison. I determined at the time that when I had my chance my gentlemen should each have a **draw** out of one of these boxes, while I ate the pill that remained. It would be quite as deadly and a good deal less noisy than firing across a handkerchief. From that day I had always my pill boxes about with me, and the time had now come when I was to use them.

"It was nearer one than twelve, and a wild, **bleak** night, blowing hard and raining in **torrents**. **Dismal** as it was outside, I was glad within—so glad that I could have shouted out from pure exultation. If any of you gentlemen have ever pined for a thing, and longed for it during twenty long years, and then suddenly found it within your reach, you would understand my feelings. I lit a cigar, and puffed at it to steady my nerves, but my hands were trembling, and my temples throbbing with excitement. As I drove, I could see old John Ferrier and sweet Lucy looking at me out of the darkness and smiling at me, just as plain as I see you all in this room. All the way they were ahead of me, one on each side of the horse until I pulled up at the house in the Brixton Road.

"There was not a soul to be seen, nor a sound to be heard, except the dripping of

bleak [bli:k] adj.
황량한, 쓸쓸한, 흐린
torrent [tɔ́:r-ənt, tár- / tɔ́r-] n.
급류, 분류, 폭발
dismal [dízməl] adj.
음울한, 쓸쓸한

the rain. When I looked in at the window, I found Drebber all huddled together in a drunken sleep. I shook him by the arm, 'It's time to get out,' I said.

"'All right, cabby,' said he.

"I suppose he thought we had come to the hotel that he had mentioned, for he got out without another word, and followed me down the garden. I had to walk beside him to keep him steady, for he was still a little **top-heavy**. When we came to the door, I opened it and led him into the front room. I give you my word that all the way, the father and the daughter were walking in front of us.

"'It's **infernally** dark,' said he, stamping about.

"'We'll soon have a light,' I said, striking a match and putting it to a wax candle which I had brought with me. 'Now, Enoch Drebber,' I continued, turning to him, and holding the light to my own face, 'who am I?'

"He gazed at me with bleared, drunken eyes for a moment, and then I saw a horror spring up in them, and convulse his whole features, which showed me

livid [lívid] adj.
창백한, 검푸른
perspiration [pə̀ːr-
spəréiʃən] n.
땀

that he knew me. He staggered back with a **livid** face, and I saw the **perspiration** break out upon his brow, while his teeth chattered in his head. At the sight I leaned my back against the door and laughed loud and long. I had always known that vengeance would be sweet, but I had never hoped for the contentment of soul which now possessed me.

"'You dog!' I said; 'I have hunted you

gush [gʌʃ] v.
세차게 흘러나오다, 쏟아져 나오다

from Salt Lake City to St. Petersburg, and you have always escaped me. Now, at last your wanderings have come to an end, for either you or I shall never see to-morrow's sun rise.' He shrunk still farther away as I spoke, and I could see on his face that he thought I was mad. So I was for the time. The pulses in my temples beat like sledge-hammers, and I believe I would have had a fit of some sort if the blood had not **gushed** from my nose and relieved me.

"'What do you think of Lucy Ferrier now?' I cried, locking the door, and shaking the key in his face. 'Punishment has been slow in coming, but it has overtaken you at last.' I saw his coward lips tremble as I spoke. He would have begged for his life, but he knew well that it was useless.

"'Would you murder me?' he stammered.

"'There is no murder,' I answered. 'Who talks of murdering a mad dog? What mercy had you upon my poor darling, when you dragged her from her slaughtered father, and bore her away to your accursed and shameless harem?'

"'It was not I who killed her father,'

he cried.

"'But it was you who broke her innocent heart,' I shrieked, thrusting the box before him. 'Let the high God judge between us. Choose and eat. There is death in one and life in the other. I shall take what you leave. Let us see if there is justice upon the earth, or if we are ruled by chance.'

"He cowered away with wild cries and prayers for mercy, but I drew my knife and held it to his throat until he had obeyed me. Then I swallowed the other, and we stood facing one another in silence for a minute or more, waiting to see which was to live and which was to die. Shall I ever forget the look which came over his face when the first warning pangs told him that the poison was in his system? I laughed as I saw it, and held Lucy's marriage ring in front of his eyes. It was but for a moment, for the action of the alkaloid is rapid. A spasm of pain contorted his features; he threw his hands out in front of him, staggered, and then, with a hoarse cry, fell heavily upon the floor. I turned him over with my foot, and placed my hand upon his heart. There was no movement. He was dead!

"The blood had been streaming from my nose, but I had taken no notice of it. I don't know what it was that put it into my head to write upon the wall with it. Perhaps it was some mischievous idea of setting the police upon a wrong track, for I felt light-hearted and cheerful. I remembered a German being found in New York with RACHE written up above him, and it was argued at the time in the newspapers that the secret societies must have done it. I guessed that what puzzled the New Yorkers would puzzle the Londoners, so I dipped my finger in my own blood and printed it on a convenient place on the wall. Then I walked down to my cab and found that there was nobody about, and that the night was still very wild. I had driven some distance, when I put my hand into the pocket in which I usually kept Lucy's ring, and found that it was not there. I was thunderstruck at this, for it was the only **memento** that I had of her. Thinking

---

memento [miméntou] n. 과거의 기억을 떠올리게 하는 것, 유품

disarm [disá:rm, diz-] v. (무장을) 해제하다, 적개심(의혹, 공포 등)을 없애다

that I might have dropped it when I stooped over Drebber's body, I drove back, and leaving my cab in a side street, I went boldly up to the house—for I was ready to dare anything rather than lose the ring. When I arrived there, I walked right into the arms of a police-officer who was coming out, and only managed to **disarm** his suspicions by pretending to be hopelessly drunk.

"That was how Enoch Drebber came to his end. All I had to do then was to do as much for Stangerson, and so pay off John Ferrier's debt. I knew that he was staying at Halliday's Private Hotel, and I hung about all day, but he never came out. I fancy that he suspected something when Drebber failed to put in an appearance. He was cunning, was Stangerson, and always on his guard. If he thought he could keep me off by staying indoors he was very much mistaken. I soon found out which was the window of his bedroom, and early next morning I took advantage of some ladders which were lying in the lane behind the hotel, and so made my way into his room in the grey of the dawn. I woke him up and told him that the hour had come when he was to answer for the life he had taken so long before. I described Drebber's death to him, and I gave him the same choice of the poisoned pills. Instead of grasping at the chance of safety which that offered him, he sprang from his bed and flew at my throat. In self-defence I stabbed him to the heart. It would have been the same in any case, for Providence would never have allowed his guilty hand to pick out anything but the poison.

"I have little more to say, and it's as well, for I am about done up. I went on cabbing it for a day or so, intending to keep at it until I could save enough to take me back to America. I was standing in the yard when a ragged youngster asked if there was a cabby there called Jefferson Hope, and said that his cab was wanted by a gentleman at 221B, Baker Street. I went round suspecting no harm, and the next thing I knew, this young man here had the bracelets on my wrists, and as neatly shackled as ever I saw in my life. That's the whole of my story,

blasé [blɑːzéi, ́-] adj.
냉담한, 무심한

jocose [dʒoukóus] adj.
익살맞은, 농담하는, 웃기는

gentlemen. You may consider me to be a murderer; but I hold that I am just as much an officer of justice as you are."

So thrilling had the man's narrative been and his manner was so impressive that we had sat silent and absorbed. Even the professional detectives, **blasé** as they were in every detail of crime, appeared to be keenly interested in the man's story. When he finished, we sat for some minutes in a stillness which was only broken by the scratching of Lestrade's pencil as he gave the finishing touches to his shorthand account.

"There is only one point on which I should like a little more information," Sherlock Holmes said at last. "Who was your accomplice who came for the ring which I advertised?"

The prisoner winked at my friend **jocosely**. "I can tell my own secrets," he said, "but I don't get other people into trouble. I saw your advertisement, and I thought it might be a plant, or it might be the ring which I wanted. My friend volunteered to go and see. I think you'll own he did it smartly."

"Not a doubt of that," said Holmes heartily.

"Now, gentlemen," the Inspector remarked gravely, "the forms of the law must be complied with. On Thursday the prisoner will be brought before the magistrates, and your attendance will be required. Until then I will be responsible for him." He rang the bell as he spoke, and Jefferson Hope was led off by a couple of warders, while my friend and I made our way out of the Station and took a cab back to Baker Street.

7 The Conclusion

testimony [téstəmòuni / -məni] n.
증언, 증거, 증명
tribunal [traibjú:nl, tri-] n.
재판소
mete [mi:t] v.
나누어 주다, 할당하다

We had all been warned to appear before the magistrates upon the Thursday; but when the Thursday came there was no occasion for our **testimony**. A higher Judge had taken the matter in hand, and Jefferson Hope had been summoned before a **tribunal** where strict justice would be **meted** out to him. On the very night after his capture the aneurism burst, and he was found in the morning stretched upon the floor of the cell, with a placid smile upon his face, as though he had been able in his dying moments to look back upon a useful life, and on work well done.

"Gregson and Lestrade will be wild about his death," Holmes remarked, as we chatted it over next evening. "Where will their grand advertisement be now?"

"I don't see that they had very much to do with his capture," I answered.

"What you do in this world is a matter of no consequence," returned my companion, bitterly. "The question is, what can you make people believe that you have done. Never mind," he continued, more brightly, after a pause. "I would not have missed the investigation for anything. There has been no better case within my recollection. Simple as it was, there were several most instructive points about it."

"Simple!" I ejaculated.

"Well, really, it can hardly be described as otherwise," said Sherlock Holmes, smiling at my surprise. "The proof of its intrinsic simplicity is, that without any help **save** a few very ordinary deductions I was able to lay my hand upon the criminal within three days."

"That is true," said I.

save [seiv] prep.
~을 제외하고

hindrance [híndrəns] n.
방해, 장애

follow [fálou / fɔ́lou] v.
이해하다
come to pass:
발생하다, 일어나다

"I have already explained to you that what is out of the common is usually a guide rather than a **hindrance**. In solving a problem of this sort, the grand thing is to be able to reason backwards. That is a very useful accomplishment, and a very easy one, but people do not practise it much. In the everyday affairs of life it is more useful to reason forwards, and so the other comes to be neglected. There are fifty who can reason synthetically for one who can reason analytically."

"I confess," said I, "that I do not quite **follow** you."

"I hardly expected that you would. Let me see if I can make it clearer. Most people, if you describe a train of events to them, will tell you what the result would be. They can put those events together in their minds, and argue from them that something will **come to pass**. There are few people, however, who, if you told them a result, would be able to evolve from their own inner consciousness what the steps were which led up to that result. This power is what I mean when I talk of reasoning backwards, or analytically."

"I understand," said I.

"Now this was a case in which you were given the result and had to find everything else for yourself. Now let me endeavour to show you the different steps in my reasoning. To begin at the beginning. I approached the house, as you know, on foot, and with my mind entirely free from all impressions. I naturally began by examining the roadway, and there, as I have already explained to you, I saw clearly the marks of a cab, which, I **ascertained** by inquiry, must have been there during the night. I satisfied myself that it was a cab and not a private carriage by the narrow gauge of the wheels. The ordinary London growler is considerably less wide than a gentleman's brougham.

"This was the first point gained. I then walked slowly down the garden path, which happened to be composed of a clay soil, peculiarly suitable for taking impressions. No doubt it appeared to you to be a mere **trampled** line of **slush**, but to my trained eyes every mark upon

---

ascertain [æ̀sərtéin] v.
확인하다, 밝혀내다

trample [trǽmp-əl] v.
짓밟다
slush [slʌʃ] n.
진창

obliterate [əblítərèit] v.
없애다

nocturnal [nɑktə́:rnl / nɔk-] adj.
밤의, 야간의

its surface had a meaning. There is no branch of detective science which is so important and so much neglected as the art of tracing footsteps. Happily, I have always laid great stress upon it, and much practice has made it second nature to me. I saw the heavy footmarks of the constables, but I saw also the track of the two men who had first passed through the garden. It was easy to tell that they had been before the others, because in places their marks had been entirely **obliterated** by the others coming upon the top of them. In this way my second link was formed, which told me that the **nocturnal** visitors were two in number, one remarkable for his height (as I calculated from the length of his stride), and the other fashionably dressed, to judge from the small and elegant impression left by his boots.

"On entering the house this last inference was confirmed. My well-booted man lay before me. The tall one, then, had done the murder, if murder there was. There was no wound upon the dead man's person, but the agitated expression upon

agitation [æ̀dʒətéiʃən] n.
불안, 동요
sniff [snif] v.
냄새를 맡다
hypothesis [haipάθəsis / -pɔ́θə-] n.
가설 (假說)
toxicologist [tὰksikάlədʒist / tɔ̀ksikɔl-] n. 독극물학자

"...By the method of exclusion, I had arrived at this result, for no other hypothesis would meet the facts..."

his face assured me that he had foreseen his fate before it came upon him. Men who die from heart disease, or any sudden natural cause, never by any chance exhibit **agitation** upon their features. Having **sniffed** the dead man's lips I detected a slightly sour smell, and I came to the conclusion that he had had poison forced upon him. Again, I argued that it had been forced upon him from the hatred and fear expressed upon his face. By the method of exclusion, I had arrived at this result, for no other **hypothesis** would meet the facts. Do not imagine that it was a very unheard-of idea. The forcible administration of poison is by no means a new thing in criminal annals. The cases of Dolsky in Odessa, and of Leturier in Montpellier, will occur at once to any **toxicologist**.

"And now came the great question as to the reason why. Robbery had not been the object of the murder, for nothing was taken. Was it politics, then, or was it a woman? That was the question which confronted me. I was inclined from the first to the latter supposition. Political

7 The Conclusion

perpetrator [pə́ːrpətrèitər] n. 가해자, 범인
inscription [inskrípʃən] n. 적힌 것, 새겨진 것
blind [blaind] n. 눈속임, 숨기는 수단

assassins are only too glad to do their work and to fly. This murder had, on the contrary, been done most deliberately, and the **perpetrator** had left his tracks all over the room, showing that he had been there all the time. It must have been a private wrong, and not a political one, which called for such a methodical revenge. When the **inscription** was discovered upon the wall, I was more inclined than ever to my opinion. The thing was too evidently a **blind**. When the ring was found, however, it settled the question. Clearly the murderer had used it to remind his victim of some dead or absent woman. It was at this point that I asked Gregson whether he had inquired in his telegram to Cleveland as to any particular point in Mr. Drebber's former career. He answered, you remember, in the negative.

"...It was at this point that I asked Gregson whether he had inquired in his telegram to Cleveland as to any particular point in Mr. Drebber's former career. .

"I then proceeded to make a careful examination of the room, which confirmed me in my opinion as to the murderer's height, and furnished me with the additional details as to the Trichinopoly cigar and the length of his nails. I had already

hazard [hǽzərd] v.
과감히 말하다, 추측하다

come to the conclusion, since there were no signs of a struggle, that the blood which covered the floor had burst from the murderer's nose in his excitement. I could perceive that the track of blood coincided with the track of his feet. It is seldom that any man, unless he is very full-blooded, breaks out in this way through emotion, so I **hazarded** the opinion that the criminal was probably a robust and ruddy-faced man. Events proved that I had judged correctly.

"Having left the house, I proceeded to do what Gregson had neglected. I telegraphed to the head of the police at Cleveland, limiting my inquiry to the circumstances connected with the marriage of Enoch Drebber. The answer was conclusive. It told me that Drebber had already applied for the protection of the law against an old rival in love, named Jefferson Hope, and that this same Hope was at present in Europe. I knew now that I held the clue to the mystery in my hand, and all that remained was to secure the murderer.

"I had already determined in my own

"... It told me that Drebber had already applied for the protection of the law against an old rival in love, named Jefferson Hope, and that this same Hope was at present in Europe..."

mind that the man who had walked into the house with Drebber was none other than the man who had driven the cab. The marks in the road showed me that the horse had wandered on in a way which would have been impossible **had there been anyone in charge of it**. Where, then, could the driver be, unless he were inside the house? Again, it is absurd to suppose that any sane man would carry out a deliberate crime under the very eyes, as it were, of a third person, who was sure to betray him. Lastly, supposing one man wished to dog another through London, what better means could he adopt than to turn cabdriver. All these considerations led me to the irresistible conclusion that Jefferson Hope was to be found among the **jarveys** of the Metropolis.

"If he had been one, there was no reason to believe that he had ceased to be. On the contrary, from his point of view, any sudden change would be likely to draw attention to himself. He would probably, for a time at least, continue to perform his duties. There was no reason to suppose that he was going under an **assumed**

---

had there been anyone in charge of it:
if there had been anyone in charge of it
jarvey [dʒáːrvi] n.
마부

assumed [əsjúːmd] adj.
가짜의, 가공의

proprietor [prəpráiətər] n.
소유자, 경영자
ferret [férit] v.
찾아내다, 발견하다
surmise [sərmáiz, sə́:r-maiz] v.
추측하다

name. Why should he change his name in a country where no one knew his original one? I therefore organized my street arab detective corps, and sent them systematically to every cab **proprietor** in London until they **ferreted** out the man that I wanted. How well they succeeded, and how quickly I took advantage of it, are still fresh in your recollection. The murder of Stangerson was an incident which was entirely unexpected, but which could hardly in any case have been prevented. Through it, as you know, I came into possession of the pills, the existence of which I had already **surmised**. You see, the whole thing is a chain of logical sequences without a break or flaw."

"It is wonderful!" I cried. "Your merits should be publicly recognized. You should publish an account of the case. If you won't, I will for you."

"You may do what you like, Doctor," he answered. "See here!" he continued, handing a paper over to me, "look at this!"

It was the *Echo* for the day, and the paragraph to which he pointed was devoted

7 The Conclusion

to the case in question.

"The public," it said, "have lost a sensational treat through the sudden death of the man Hope, who was suspected of the murder of Mr. Enoch Drebber and of Mr. Joseph Stangerson. The details of the case will probably be never known now, though we are informed upon good authority that the crime was the result of an old-standing and romantic **feud**, in which love and Mormonism bore a part. It seems that both the victims belonged, in their younger days, to the Latter Day Saints, and Hope, the deceased prisoner, **hails** also **from** Salt Lake City. If the case has had no other effect, it, at least, brings out in the most striking manner the efficiency of our detective police force, and will serve as a lesson to all foreigners that they will do wisely to settle their feuds at home, and not to carry them on to British **soil**. It is an open secret that the credit of this smart capture belongs entirely to the well-known Scotland Yard officials, **Messrs.** Lestrade and Gregson. The man was **apprehended**, it appears, in the rooms of a certain Mr. Sherlock

---

feud [fju:d] n.
불화, 반목
hail from: come from, ~출신이다
soil [sɔil] n.
나라, 국토
Messrs. [mésərz] n.
Mr.의 복수
apprehend [æprihénd] v.
체포하다, 구금하다

attain [ətéin] v.
얻다, 달성하다
testimonial
[tèstəmóuniəl] n.
표창장, 감사장

Holmes, who has himself, as an amateur, shown some talent in the detective line, and who, with such instructors, may hope in time to **attain** to some degree of their skill. It is expected that a **testimonial** of some sort will be presented to the two officers as a fitting recognition of their services."

"Didn't I tell you so when we started?" cried Sherlock Holmes with a laugh. "That's

the result of all our Study in Scarlet: to get them a testimonial!"

"Never mind," I answered, "I have all the facts in my journal, and the public shall know them. In the meantime you must make yourself contented by the consciousness of success, like the Roman miser—

"'Populus me sibilat, at mihi plaudo
   Ipse domi simul ac nummos contemplor in arca.'"

> "'Populus me sibilat...: 호레이스의 아포리즘(경구) "사람들이 나를 힐난할지라도, 금고에 모아둔 돈을 보며 홀로 만족하겠네."

주홍색 연구 시놉시스

제 1 부
육군 군의관 존 H. 왓슨 박사의 회고록 재판(再版)

1. 미스터 셜록 홈즈

왓슨이 군의관이 되기 위한 의학 공부를 마치고, 인도의 한 연대에 배속되며, 2차 아프가니스탄 전쟁이 발발한다.

왓슨이 불운의 마이완드 전투에 참전해서, 어깨에 지자일 탄환에 의한 부상을 당한다. 살기등등한 무슬림 군인인 가지즈(Ghazis)에게 붙잡힐 위기에 처하지만, 부하 병사인 머리의 도움을 받아 적에게서 탈출한다.

왓슨이 페샤와르에 있는 기지 병원으로 후송되어 건강을 회복한다. 이번에는 장티푸스에 걸리고, 수 개월간 사경을 헤매게 된다. 그가 다시 건강을 되찾게 되자, 의료위원회에서는 그를 귀국시키기로 결정한다.

왓슨이 영국으로 돌아와 런던의 한 호텔에 머문다. 이내 재정적 어려움을 겪게 되고, 덜 화려하고 값싼 주거지로 옮기기로 마음먹는다.

왓슨이 크라이티리언 바 앞에서 이전에 자신의 조수로 일했던 스탬포드를 우연히 만나고, 그에게 점심을 같이하자고 한다. 왓슨이 다른 주거지로 옮기

려는 자신의 생각을 말하자, 스탬포드는 셜록 홈즈라는 인물이 같은 고민을 하고 있다고 얘기한다. 왓슨이 그를 만나고 싶어 하고, 둘은 그가 일한다는 병원으로 향한다.

병원으로 가는 중에 스탬포드가 셜록 홈즈의 기이한 점을 얘기한다.

병원의 화학실험실에서 범죄 수사에 유용한 시약을 발견하여 기뻐하고 있는 홈즈를 스탬포드가 왓슨에게 소개한다.

홈즈가 왓슨을 보자마자 그가 아프가니스탄에서 왔음을 언급하여 왓슨을 놀라게 한다.

스탬포드가 홈즈에게 그들이 온 이유를 얘기한다. 홈즈는 왓슨과 주거비를 나눌 수 있게 되어 기뻐하고, 베이커 거리에 그가 봐둔 적당한 집이 있다고 말한다. 둘은 다음날 정오에 만날 약속을 한다.

호텔로 돌아가는 길에, 왓슨은 홈즈가 어떻게 그가 아프가니스탄에서 온 사실을 알게 되었는지 신기해한다.

2. 추리의 과학

왓슨과 홈즈가 베이커 가 街221B 번지를 방문한다. 계약이 바로 성사되고, 그들은 새 주거지로 이사한다.

왓슨이 홈즈의 기이한 생활방식에 흥미를 갖게 되고, 별난 분야에 관한 그의 지식에 놀란다.

왓슨은 또한 홈즈의 무지함이 그의 지식만큼이나 대단함을 알게 된다. 그는 홈즈가 토머스 칼라일도 태양계에 대해서도 모르고 있음을 발견한다. 홈즈는 인간의 두뇌를 물건을 체계적으로 두어야 하는 빈 다락방에 비유한다.

왓슨이 홈즈의 지식과 기술 등을 종이에 적어서 홈즈가 하는 일이 무언지를 알아내려 하지만, 결국 포기한다.

많은 다양한 사람들이 홈즈의 자문을 받기 위해 방문한다. 왓슨이 홈즈의 직업이 무엇인지 궁금해한다.

　어느 날 아침, 왓슨이 테이블 위에 놓인 잡지에서 추리와 분석의 과학에 대한 기사를 읽게 된다. 왓슨은 그 기사 내용에 수긍하지 않으며, 말도 안 되는 소리라고 깎아내린다. 홈즈가 그 기사를 쓴 사람이 바로 자신이라고 얘기한다. 홈즈가 본인이 자문 탐정임을 얘기하고, 왓슨이 아프가니스탄에서 온 사실을 알게 된 경위를 설명한다.

　왓슨이 홈즈의 오만한 대화 방식에 기분이 상하게 되는데, 집 주소를 살피며 길 건너편을 걷고 있는 한 남자를 발견한다. 왓슨이 그 남자가 뭘 찾고 있는지 의아해한다. 홈즈가 그 사내는 퇴역한 해병 부사관이라고 말한다. 왓슨이 홈즈가 그의 말을 확인할 방법이 없어서 허풍을 친다고 생각한다.

　그 길가의 사내는 마침 홈즈에게 편지를 전하기 위해 온 사람이었으며, 그가 방으로 와서 홈즈에게 편지를 전달한다.

　왓슨은 오만한 홈즈에게 굴욕을 안길 기회가 왔음을 직감하고, 그 편지 배달인에게 그의 이전 직업이 무엇이었는지를 묻는다. 왓슨의 예상과 달리, 홈즈의 추리가 옳았음을 알게 된다.

3. 로리스턴 가든 미스터리

　그 배달인이 퇴역한 해병 부사관이라는 사실을 어떻게 알게 되었는지를 홈즈가 왓슨에게 설명한다.

　홈즈의 편지는 런던경찰청의 그렉슨 형사가 보낸 것으로, 왓슨이 홈즈에게 편지를 읽어준다.

　편지에 따르면, 미국 오하이오 주 클리블랜드에서 온 이녹 J. 드레버라는 인물이 로리스턴 가든의 한 빈집에서 사망한 것을 간밤에 순찰 중이던 순경이 발견했다고 한다. 또한 방안에 핏자국들이 있으나, 사망자의 몸엔 아무런 상처도 없다고 한다. 그렉슨이 로리스턴 가든의 미스터리를 풀기 위해 도움을 요

청한다.

그렉슨과 레스트레이드가 런던경찰청의 민첩하고 열정적인 일급 형사들이며, 서로에게 라이벌 의식을 갖고 있다고 홈즈가 왓슨에게 알려준다. 홈즈가 왓슨에게 같이 가자고 제의한다.

안개 낀 흐린 아침 시간에 그들은 로리스턴 가든 3번가로 향한다. 사건 현장에 도착해서, 홈즈는 집 주변을 조사한다.

그렉슨이 홈즈와 왓슨을 반갑게 맞는다. 홈즈가 그렉슨에게 그 또는 레스트레이드가 마차를 타고 오지 않았는지 묻는다. 그렉슨은 아니라고 답한다.

왓슨이 방안에 움직임 없는 섬뜩한 피해자의 모습과 그의 얼굴에 나타난 공포와 증오의 표정을 보고 충격을 받는다. 레스트레이드가 나타나 홈즈와 왓슨에게 인사한다. 그는 아무 단서도 찾을 수 없음을 불평한다.

홈즈가 방안의 여러 핏자국을 가리키며 사망자에게 아무 상처가 없는 게 확실한지 묻는다. 그는 핏자국을 제2의 인물, 아마도 가해자의 것으로 추정한다. 홈즈가 사망자의 입가를 냄새 맡고, 에나멜가죽 구두 밑창을 들여다본다.

사망자가 들것에 실려 나갈 때 반지 하나가 떨어져 굴러간다. 레스트레이드가 반지를 집어 들고 여자의 결혼반지임을 확인한다. 그렉슨이 문제가 더 복잡해졌다고 하지만, 홈즈는 달리 생각한다.

드레버의 주머니에서 발견된 서류로부터, 드레버에게 이후에 그의 비서로 밝혀지는 스탠거슨이라는 동료가 있었고, 그들이 뉴욕으로 돌아갈 예정이었음을 알게 된다.

홈즈가 그렉슨에게 스탠거슨이라는 인물과 클리블랜드에 관한 조사를 했는지 묻는다. 그렉슨이 조사를 바로 했으며, 오늘 아침 클리블랜드로 전보를 쳤다고 말한다. 그러나 홈즈는 그렉슨의 전보 내용에 만족하지 못한다.

레스트레이드가 벽에 피로 쓰인 RACHE라는 글자를 발견한다. 레스트레이드는 이 글자를 범인이 자신의 피로 쓴 것으로 추정하고, 레이첼 Rachel이라는 여성이 관련되었을 것으로 추측한다.

홈즈가 사건현장을 몇 분 정도 조사하고, 어젯밤 사망자를 발견한 순경에 대해 묻는다. 레스트레이드가 케닝턴 파크 게이트, 오들리 코트 46번지에 사는 존 랜스라고 알려준다.

사건현장을 떠나기 전에, 홈즈가 레스트레이드와 그렉슨에게 범인의 인상착의를 말하고, 드레버가 독살되었음을 알려준다. 또한, RACHE라는 글자가 여성의 이름이 아니라 복수를 의미하는 독일어라고 말한다.

4. 존 랜스의 증언

왓슨과 홈즈가 가까운 전신국에 들르고, 홈즈가 장문의 전보를 친다.

존 랜스에게 가는 도중에 홈즈가 왓슨에게 범인의 인상착의와 다른 세부 사항을 알게 된 경위를 설명한다. 홈즈가 마차의 바퀴 자국으로부터 두 사람이 어젯밤 그 빈집에 왔음을 추론한다. 홈즈는 길에 나 있는 에나멜가죽 구두와 코가 각진 구두의 발자국을 발견하는데, 이는 드레버와 용의자로 추정되는 또 다른 인물의 것임을 나타낸다. 또한 그는 코가 각진 구두의 발자국으로부터 용의자의 키와 나이 등을 추리한다. 그리고 벽에 쓰인 RACHE라는 글자는 독일인이 쓴 것이 아니며, 단지 사회주의나 비밀결사 등을 암시하여 경찰 수사에 혼선을 주기 위한 속임수에 불과하다고 말한다.

그들이 추가 정보를 얻기 위해 랜스 순경의 집에 이른다. 랜스가 어젯밤 그가 겪은 일을 얘기한다.

순찰 중에 랜스는 그 빈집에 불이 켜져 있는 것을 보게 됐다. 무언가 수상함을 느껴서 랜스가 그 집에 가게 되고, 방에서 죽어있는 드레버를 발견했다.

랜스가 대문으로 다시 달려가 휘슬을 불어 동료들을 불렀는데, 그곳에서 어느 술에 취한 주정뱅이가 난간에 기대어 목청껏 노래를 불러대고 있었다.

랜스는 그를 대수롭지 않게 여겼지만, 그는 사실 범죄를 저지른 자였으며, 술 취

한 척 연기하여 순경의 의심을 피한 것이었다. 랜스 순경이 그를 체포하는 데 실패하여 놓아주게 됐다.

홈즈는 그 사내가 사건 현장에 실수로 떨어뜨린 여자의 결혼반지를 되찾으러 돌아왔음을 확신한다. 홈즈는 그 결혼반지를 미끼로 해서 그를 잡기로 결심한다.

5. 우리의 광고를 보고 방문객이 오다

홈즈가 왓슨에게 그가 모든 신문에 낸 광고를 보여주는데, 금으로 된 결혼반지를 주웠으며, 반지의 주인은 베이커 가 221B로 찾으러 오라는 내용의 광고이다.

홈즈와 왓슨이 그들의 거처로 범인 또는 그의 공범이 올 것을 기대한다.

건장한 체격의 남자를 기대했으나, 예상과는 달리 늙고 주름진 여성이 방문한다. 그녀는 그 반지가 자기 딸의 것이라고 주장한다. 왓슨이 홈즈가 미리 준비한 문제의 반지와 유사한 반지를 그녀에게 건네준다. 그녀가 방을 나가자마자, 그녀를 공범으로 의심하는 홈즈가 뒤따라 나간다.

홈즈가 밤늦게 집으로 돌아와서, 왓슨에게 자신의 실패담을 들려준다.

노파가 마차에 타자마자 홈즈가 마차의 뒤에 올라탔다.

노파가 말한 목적지에 도착했을 때, 홈즈와 마차의 마부는 그녀가 공기 중으로 사라진 것을 발견했다.

그 노파는 실제로는 활동적이고 변장에도 능한 젊은 남자였으며, 홈즈의 미행을 눈치채고 마차가 목적지로 가는 도중에 마차에서 뛰어내린 것이다.

그들이 쫓는 사내는 생각보다 외로운 존재가 아니며, 그를 위해 위험을 감수할 친구를 가진 게 분명했다.

6. 토비아스 그렉슨이 능력을 발휘하다

홈즈와 왓슨이 아침을 먹으며 로리스턴 미스터리에 관한 신문 기사를 읽는다. 그들은 신문에서 드레버가 샤펜티어 부인의 하숙집에서 그의 비서인 스탠거슨과 함께 머물렀음을 알게 된다. 드레버와 스탠거슨은 화요일에 하숙집을 떠나 리버풀행 특급열차를 타기 위해 유스턴 역으로 출발했다. 역 플랫폼에 있는 그들을 누군가가 목격했으나, 드레버가 그 빈집에서 사망한 채로 발견되기까지 그들의 행적은 알려진 게 없다.

난데없이 거리의 부랑아들 여섯 명이 방안으로 몰려와 왓슨을 놀라게 한다. 그들은 사건을 조사하기 위해 홈즈가 고용한 베이커가 수사대이다. 아이들은 임금을 지급받고 그들의 조사를 계속하기 위해 방을 나간다.

그렉슨이 홈즈에게 아서 샤펜티어라는 용의자를 체포했다고 알리기 위해 찾아온다. 그렉슨이 스탠거슨을 쫓고 있는 그의 경쟁자 레스트레이드를 비웃는데, 레스트레이드가 어리석은 시도를 하고 있다고 생각하기 때문이다. 그렉슨이 용의자를 체포한 경위를 얘기한다.

그렉슨이 사건 현장에 떨어진 모자를 추적하여, 드레버와 스랜거슨이 머물렀던 샤펜리어 부인의 하숙집을 찾아갔다. 그렉슨이 드레버와 스랜거슨에 관해 샤펜리어 부인에게 물었다.

샤펜리어 부인은 그녀의 정직한 딸 앨리스가 진실을 말할 것을 주장하여 그렉슨에게 사실을 얘기하게 되었다.

거칠고 야만적인 드레버가 앨리스를 좋아하게 되었는데, 한번은 드레버가 앨리스를 붙잡고 부둥켜안기까지 하였다. 샤펜리어 부인은 이를 계기로 드레버에게 집을 나가 줄 것을 통보하게 되었다.

드레버와 스탠거슨이 그날 아침 여덟 시에 떠났지만, 한 시간도 안 되어 드레버가 돌아왔다. 무척이나 흥분되고 술에 취한 상태의 드레버가 앨리스에게 자기와 같이 떠나자고 유혹했다. 앨리스가 무서운 나머지 그에게서 멀어지려 했다. 드레버가 앨리스의 손목을 잡고 문가로 끌고 가며 강제로 납치하려고 했다.

샤펜티어 부인이 비명을 질렀는데, 이때 아들인 아서가 방으로 들어왔다. 샤펜티어 부인이 겁에 질려 머리를 들지 못했고, 욕설과 거친 격투의 소리를 들었다. 그녀가 고개를 들어 보니, 아서가 몽둥이를 손에 들고 문가에 서서 웃고 있었다.

아서가 악당 드레버가 무슨 짓을 벌일지 보기 위해 그를 뒤쫓았다.

그렉슨은 아서가 드레버와 싸웠으며 그를 쫓아갔다는 이유로 아서가 있는 곳을 찾아 그를 주요 피의자로 체포했다.

그렉슨이 스탠거슨의 행방을 쫓고 있는 레스트레이드를 비웃으며 재미있어 하는데, 레스트레이드가 지치고 괴로운 표정을 하며 방에 나타난다.

레스트레이드가 스탠거슨이 오늘 아침 할리데이 프라이빗 호텔에서 살해되었다고 말한다.

7. 어둠 속의 빛

레스트레이드가 스탠거슨을 뒤쫓은 얘기를 들려준다.

레스트레이드는 스탠거슨이 드레버의 죽음과 관련이 있다고 믿었다.

드레버와 스탠거슨이 유스턴 역에 같이 있는 것이 목격되었으므로, 레스트레이드는 스탠거슨이 역 주변 어딘가에 머물러 있을 것이라고 추측했다.

레스트레이드가 역 근처의 호텔들을 하나하나 찾아갔는데, 시행착오 끝에 스탠거슨이 머물고 있는 할리데이 프라이빗 호텔에 이르게 되었다.

놀랍게도 레스트레이드는 스탠거슨이 그의 방에서 칼에 찔려 죽어있고, 사망자의 위에 피로 쓰인 RACHE라는 글을 발견하게 되었다.

레스트레이드가 창턱에 놓인 2개의 알약을 담은 작은 상자를 발견했다.

홈즈는 그 상자가 드레버의 죽음과 관련이 있다고 생각한다. 홈즈가 왓슨에게 아래층에서 병들어 신음하고 있어 안락사가 필요한 테리어를 가져와달라고 부탁한다.

홈즈가 하나의 알약을 칼로 반으로 잘라내어, 그중 하나를 우유에 섞어 개에게 먹인다. 그러나 개는 아무런 반응도 보이지 않는다. 순간 실망을 하지만, 홈즈는 또 다른 가능성을 생각해낸다. 홈즈가 두 번째 알약을 먹여보자, 고통스러워하던 개가 평안한 안식을 갖게 되는데, 따라서 하나의 알약은 맹독이지만 다른 하나는 전혀 무해한 것으로 판명된다.

왓슨과 두 명의 형사는 홈즈에게 사건의 진상을 얘기해달라고 채근한다.

거리 부랑아들의 대표인 위긴스가 방으로 와서 아래에 마차가 도착했다고 보고한다. 홈즈가 형사들에게 수갑을 꺼내 보이며 런던 경찰청에서 이 도구를 쓰지 않는 이유를 궁금해한다. 홈즈가 위긴스에게 아래층의 마부에게 올라와서 자신이 짐 싸는 걸 도와달라고 할 것을 지시한다.

홈즈가 작은 여행 가방을 꺼내어 묶기 시작하는데, 이때 마부가 방으로 들어온다. 몸을 낮춰 일에 열중하며 절대 고개를 돌리지 않은 상태로 홈즈가 마부에게 여행 가방 잠그는 걸 도와달라고 말한다.

마부가 다소 불만 섞인 태도로 와서 돕기 위해 두 손을 아래로 내린다. 이때 홈즈가 그에게 수갑을 채우며, 이 마부가 그들이 찾는 인물인 제퍼슨 호프임을 밝힌다.

순간적으로 모두가 황망함에 마치 돌이 되어버린 듯 굳어버린다. 이때 분노의 함성을 지르며 마부가 창문을 뚫고 탈출을 시도하지만, 두 명의 형사와 홈즈가 그에게 달려든다. 마부와의 치열한 난투 끝에, 마침내 그를 체포한다.

제 2 부
성인(聖人)들의 나라

1. 알칼리 대평원에서

이야기는 1847년 북아메리카 중앙지대로 되돌아간다.

시에라 블랑코의 외로운 여행자인 존 페리어는 물을 찾지 못해 절망에 빠져 있다. 그의 눈앞으로는 거대한 소금 평원이 펼쳐져 있을 뿐이다. 이 거대한 평원 어디에도 희망의 빛은 보이지 않는다. 그는 죽음의 문턱에 와 있음을 예감하는데, 물이 이미 다 떨어졌고 강도 찾지 못했기 때문이다.

페리어는 루시라는 아이와 동행하고 있는데, 그들은 일행 중 유일한 생존자들이다. 그들은 여행 도중 아이의 어머니를 포함한 모든 사람을 잃었다.

페리어가 루시에게 기도해달라고 부탁하고, 그들은 함께 신의 자비와 용서를 구하는 기도를 드린다. 기도 후에 그들은 커다란 돌의 그늘에 자리하며, 곧 꿈도 없는 깊은 잠에 빠져든다.

페리어와 루시는 안식처를 찾아 여행 중인 여행자들에게 발견되어 구조된다. 페리어는 그들이 모르몬 교도들임을 알게 된다. 페리어가 그들의 선지자인 브리검 영에게 인도된다.

브리검 영이 그들의 교리를 따르는 조건으로 페리어에게 자신들과 동행할 것을 제의한다. 페리어가 이를 수락하고, 루시가 자신이 입양한 딸임을 주장한다.

2. 유타의 꽃

모르몬 교도들이 솔트레이크 시티에 정착하고, 페리어가 밤낮으로 일하여 부를 일군다.

루시 페리어가 자라나서 아버지 페리어의 일을 돕는다. 해가 감에 따라 그녀는 더욱 크고 강하게 성장하며, 매력적인 여성으로 자란다.

어느 따스한 유월 아침, 루시가 아버지가 맡긴 일을 하러 시내에 가게 된다. 그녀가 시 외곽에 이르러 보니, 대여섯 명의 우락부락한 목동들이 모는 수많은 소 떼에 의해 길이 막혀 있다. 루시가 조바심에 자신이 탄 말을 재촉하여 빈틈으로 보이는 데로 들어갔으나, 긴 뿔의 사나운 눈빛을 가진 소 떼 안에 갇혀버린다.

소 떼의 무리에서 벗어나기 위해 그녀의 말을 이리저리 몰아본다. 불행히도 소 중에 하나의 뿔이 말의 옆구리를 거칠게 들이받아, 말은 미친 듯이 흥분한다. 말이 분노의 울음소리를 내고 뒷발로 섰으며, 이리저리 날뛴다. 루시는 승마에 숙련되어 낙마를 모면한다. 그러나 상황은 참으로 위급하다. 소들의 뿔이 그녀의 말을 계속해서 부딪치게 되고, 말은 더욱 미쳐 날뛰게 된다. 말에서 떨어지게 되면 거칠고 겁에 질린 소 떼의 발굽에 밟혀 끔찍한 죽음을 맞게 될 것이다.

이때 한 남자가 다가와 루시를 위험에서 구한다. 그가 겁에 질린 말의 재갈을 잡더니 소 떼를 헤쳐나간다. 그들이 안전한 곳에 이르자 그가 루시에게 다치지 않았는지 묻는다. 그는 큰 키에 험상궂은 얼굴의 젊은이이며, 자신을 제퍼슨 호프라고 소개한다. 루시가 자신을 구해준 것에 고마워하며, 그를 집으로 초대한다.

제퍼슨 호프는 그날 밤 존 페리어를 찾아가고, 이후로 여러 차례의 방문이 이어진다. 그는 존 페리어와의 친분을 쌓게 되고, 날이 감에 따라 그와 루시는 서로를 사랑하게 된다.

어느 날, 제퍼슨 호프는 일 문제로 루시를 떠나게 된다. 그는 두세 달 후 돌아와 루시와 결혼할 것을 약속한다.

3. 존 페리어, 선지자와 대화하다

제퍼슨 호프가 솔트레이크시티를 떠난 지 3주가 지났다. 존 페리어는 젊은

이가 돌아오고 자신의 딸을 잃는 것이 행복하지만은 않다.

페리어는 딸을 모르몬 교도와 결혼시키지 않을 결심을 항상 하고 있다. 그 문제에 관해서는 입을 다물고 있어야 하는데, 이단의 사상을 밝히는 것은 무척이나 위험한 노릇이기 때문이다.

어느 날 아침, 모르몬 교도의 지도자인 브리검 영이 페리어를 찾아오고, 그의 딸 루시가 장로들의 아들인 드레버 또는 스탠거슨과 결혼해야 한다고 주장한다.

페리어는 딸이 아직 어리므로 영에게 시간을 달라고 한다. 영이 페리어에게 한 달 내에 이를 숙고하고 그녀의 배우자를 결정하라고 말한다. 브리검 영이 떠나면서 모르몬 교리를 어기지 말 것을 위협적으로 경고한다.

브리검 영이 간 후, 페리어는 절망에 빠지게 되는데, 모르몬교의 일부다처제 교리를 수긍하지 못하기 때문이다. 브리검 영의 목소리가 집안 전체에 울려 퍼져서, 루시도 페리어와 영 사이의 대화를 듣게 된다. 페리어는 루시에게 유타를 떠나기로 한 자신의 결심을 얘기한다.

4. 필사의 탈출

이튿날 아침, 존 페리어가 솔트레이크시티에 가서, 제퍼슨 호프에게 곧바로 돌아와 자신들의 임박한 위험으로부터 탈출하도록 도와달라는 내용의 편지를 보낸다.

페리어가 집에 와 보니, 두 명의 젊은이들이 자신의 거실을 차지하고 있는 걸 보고 놀라게 된다. 그들은 드레버와 스탠거슨으로, 루시에게 청혼하러 온 것이다.

그들이 페리어 앞에서 루시 문제로 왈가왈부 논쟁을 하게 되는데, 이를 본 페리어가 분노하게 된다. 페리어가 그들을 위협하여 집에서 내쫓는다. 그들이 서둘러 줄행랑을 친다.

이튿날 아침, 페리어가 침대보에 핀으로 고정된 종이를 보게 되는데, 개심改

心하기까지의 기한이 29일 남았음을 통보하는 내용이다. 매일 남은 기일을 나타내는 불길한 표시가 집 주변에 나타나 페리어를 괴롭힌다.

호프가 마침내 마지막 날 전날에 돌아와 페리어 모녀에게 떠날 준비를 하게 한다. 앞쪽과 뒤쪽의 출입구를 모르몬 교도들이 감시하고 있어서, 옆쪽 창문을 통해 집을 나서고 들판을 가로지른다. 일행은 산길을 따라 걸음을 서두른다.

그들이 한 고갯길에서 어느 감시자의 검문을 받는다. 도중에 우연히 들은 그들의 암호를 대답하여 감시초소를 벗어난다.

5. 복수의 천사

가져온 식량이 떨어짐에 따라, 호프가 페리어 부녀와 헤어져 사냥을 떠난다. 그가 사냥을 끝내고 돌아올 때 길을 잃어버리고, 맞는 길을 찾기까지 시간을 허비한다.

호프가 사냥감을 지고 되돌아와 보니, 되는대로 만들어진 무덤과 존 페리어의 묘비명을 마주하게 된다. 황급히 주위를 둘러보나, 또 다른 무덤은 보이지 않는다. 그 사악한 추적자들이 루시를 원래 운명이었던 장로 아들의 아내들 중 하나로 삼기 위해 데려간 것이 분명하다. 그는 남은 인생을 복수에 바치기로 결심한다.

호프는 6일간을 걸어 모르몬의 도시로 돌아온다. 모르몬 친구를 한 명 만나게 되고, 그로부터 스탠거슨이 산에서 페리어를 총으로 쐈으며, 루시가 어제 드레버와 결혼한 사실을 알게 된다.

가엾은 루시는 한 달 후 슬픔에 겨운 나머지 세상을 떠나고 만다. 루시의 장례식 전날 밤, 호프가 마지막 작별인사를 하기 위해 관 앞으로 온다. 그녀의 손에서 결혼반지를 빼내는데, 그녀가 그 반지와 같이 묻히는 걸 용납할 수가 없기 때문이다.

호프는 맹렬한 불길의 복수의 열망을 품게 되고, 드레버와 스탠거슨에 대한

응징을 하고자 한다. 그는 오하이오주의 클리블랜드에서 유럽으로, 그리고 결국 런던에 이르기까지 그들에 대한 추격을 계속한다.

6. 존 왓슨 박사의 회상 뒷이야기

왓슨 박사가 이야기를 이어간다.

그들이 체포된 범인을 경찰서로 이송한다.

호프가 사건의 진상을 자진해서 말하고자 하는데, 그에게는 살날이 얼마 남지 않았기 때문이다. 왓슨이 그의 가슴을 진찰해보는데, 대동맥에 이상이 있음을 발견하고 놀란다.

호프가 자신의 이야기를 들려준다.

호프가 두 명의 원수를 런던에서 찾아냈고, 마부로 취직을 했다.

호프가 그날 드레버와 스탠거슨이 유스턴 역에 있는 걸 목격했다. 그는 그들이 열차를 놓쳤으며, 스탠거슨이 할리데이 프라이빗 호텔에 머물 거라는 사실을 알게 되었다.

호프가 드레버를 미행했는데, 드레버는 샤펜티어 부인의 집으로 되돌아갔다. 드레버가 집으로 들어가고, 호프가 밖에서 15분 정도 기다렸다.

그때, 호프는 드레버가 앨리스에게 저지른 사나운 행동으로 인해 아서에 의해 집 밖으로 내쫓기는 걸 보게 되었다.

드레버가 무심결에 호프의 마차에 타게 되며, 할리데이 프라이빗 호텔로 가자고 했다. 호프가 수염을 기른 상태여서 드레버는 호프를 알아보지 못했다. 드레버가 도중에 술집에 들러 술에 취하게 되었다. 호프가 술 취한 드레버를 태우고 미리 봐둔 브릭스턴 가의 빈집으로 마차를 몰았다.

빈집 안에서 호프가 그의 정체를 밝히고, 드레버가 경악했다.

호프가 드레버에게 강요하여 두 알약 중 하나를 선택하게 했다. 알약 중 하나는 무해하며 다른 하나는 독이 들었는데, 호프는 신이 올바른 판단을 하리라 믿었다. 드레버가 마지못해 두려워하며 하나의 알약을 먹고, 호프가 다른 하나를 먹었다.

치명적인 알약을 먹은 사람은 드레버였으며, 그가 사망에 이르렀다. 호프가 흥분한 나머지 코피를 흘리게 되는데, 자신의 피로 벽에 RACHE란 글자를 써서 경찰 수사에 혼선을 주려고 했다.

호프가 돌아가는 길에 루시의 반지를 빈집에 떨어뜨린 걸 알아차렸다. 빈집에 돌아와 보니, 이미 랜스 순경과 그의 동료들이 있는 걸 발견했다. 호프는 고주망태로 취한 척 연기를 하여 경찰의 의심을 피했다.

다음으로 호프는 존 페리어의 복수를 위해 스탠거슨에게로 갔다. 그는 스탠거슨이 머무는 할리데이 프라이빗 호텔 침실 창문을 곧바로 찾아냈다. 새벽녘에 창문을 통해 침실로 들어섰다. 스탠거슨은 알약을 선택하라는 호프의 제의를 거절하고 호프를 공격하지만, 도리어 호프에 의해 죽게 되었다.

그의 복수가 끝나서 미국으로 돌아갈 결심을 하게 되었다. 어느 날 남루한 행색의 아이가 와서 그의 이름을 가진 마부를 찾아서는 베이커가 221B의 한 신사가 그를 찾는다고 말했다. 호프는 셜록 홈즈에 의해 체포되기 전까지 아무런 위험을 의심하지 못했다.

호프의 이야기가 끝나고, 홈즈가 호프에게 늙은 여성으로 변장하여 그가 신문에 광고한 반지를 찾고 그를 따돌린 친구에 관해 묻는다. 호프는 그의 친구가 곤경에 처하길 원치 않으며, 그를 위해 자진해서 결혼반지를 찾아 준 친구의 정체를 밝히길 거부한다.

7. 결말

호프가 이튿날 아침 사망한 채로 발견되는데, 그가 수감된 날 밤 그의 대동맥이 파열했기 때문이다.

이튿날 저녁 홈즈와 왓슨이 사건에 관해 얘기한다. 어떻게 사인이 독살인지를 알게 되었고, 사건 현장의 두 개의 발자국 중 하나가 범인의 것임을 알았으며, 범인의 이름과 직업을 알게 되었고, 베이커가 수사대를 동원하여 제퍼슨 호프를 찾아냈는지 등을 홈즈가 왓슨에게 설명한다.

홈즈가 왓슨에게 신문을 하나 건네는데, 홈즈가 예상한 대로 모든 공적이 레스트레이드와 그렉슨에게 돌아갔다는 내용이다. 왓슨이 사건에 관해 기록한 모든 사실을 공개하겠다고 홈즈에게 말한다.